Goodness over Greatness

A Counterintuitive Mindset that Unlocks Fulfillment, Freedom, and Sustainable Success

Goodness over Greatness

A Counterintuitive Mindset that Unlocks Fulfillment, Freedom, and Sustainable Success

Erik Reagan

ethos
collective

Printed in the United States of America

Published by Igniting Souls
PO Box 43, Powell, OH 43065
IgnitingSouls.com

LCCN: 2024927018
Paperback ISBN: 978-1-63680-439-2
Hardback ISBN: 978-1-63680-440-8
eBook ISBN: 978-1-63680-441-5

Available in paperback, hardcover, e-book, and audiobook.

All Scripture quotations, unless otherwise indicated, are taken from the Holy Bible, New International Version®, NIV®. Copyright © 1973, 1978, 1984, 2011 by Biblica, Inc.™ Used by permission of Zondervan. All rights reserved worldwide. www.zondervan.com The "NIV" and "New International Version" are trademarks registered in the United States Patent and Trademark Office by Biblica, Inc.™

Any Internet addresses (websites, blogs, etc.) and telephone numbers printed in this book are offered as a resource. They are not intended in any way to be or imply an endorsement by Igniting Souls, nor does Igniting Souls vouch for the content of these sites and numbers for the life of this book.

Some names and identifying details may have been changed to protect the privacy of individuals.

The superscript symbol IP listed throughout this book is known as the unique certification mark created and owned by Instant IP™. Its use signifies that the corresponding expression (words, phrases, chart, graph, etc.) has been protected by Instant IP™ via smart contract. Instant IP™ is designed with the patented smart contract solution (US Patent: 11,928,748), which creates an immutable time-stamped first layer and fast layer identifying the moment in time an idea is filed on the blockchain. This solution can be used in defending intellectual property protection. Infringing upon the respective intellectual property, i.e., IP, is subject to and punishable in a court of law.

For my dad, Dale, and my father-in-law, Stephen.
Thank you for your love and support.
We lost you both too early.
I'm grateful for you — always.

TABLE OF CONTENTS

IT STARTS WITH ME

Only I can change my life.
No one can do it for me.

—Carol Burnett

My partner and I had no business experience when we started our branding agency, Focus Lab. In fact, 1 didn't even have a college degree. Despite our limited skills, our endeavor grew quickly. Over the first seven years, we hired a team, brought on a third partner, and created a structured organization with me at the helm as CEO. As we transitioned, our leadership team also strategically narrowed the focus of our business, removing the primary service I personally provided in our early years (writing code for clients). Looking back to that move, I can safely say we made the right decision. Unfortunately, less than a year after the shift, I realized I led a company that specialized in branding, and I just didn't get fired up about branding.

My first instinct was to dive deeper into the subject. To be a great CEO, I figured I simply needed to immerse myself in the craft so I could become passionate about it. Isn't that what great leaders do?

The Pursuit

Many aspire to be leaders. But I wonder if everyone who dreams about the position also wants to influence, inspire, and guide others through their actions and examples. Do they seek greatness for the sake of being a big shot, or do they want to empower others while remaining grounded in their own values, balancing ambition with compassion and humility? Leadership comes with great responsibility. I especially like the simplicity of John Maxwell's definition: "Leadership is influence. Nothing more and nothing less."[1]

In the movie *Black Panther*, T'Chaka speaks to his son T'Challa in the spiritual realm, "the Ancestral Plane," as the younger takes the throne, "You're a good man with a good heart. And it is hard for a good man to be king." Many quotes from the Marvel Cinematic Universe make a similar point. Why do so many seem to sacrifice goodness when they reach a position of greatness?

In my own journey of goodness, it didn't take long for me to decide the company's revised focus needed a new leader. I met with my co-founder and told him I thought he was the right person for the CEO position this run.

The next year, 2020, became my CEO swansong as I navigated our team through COVID and then quietly moved into the position of COO. I didn't need to love branding to create an excellent operations team. After a few months, we told our staff, and we announced the change to the world as we completed the transition.

> Why do so many seem to sacrifice goodness when they reach a position of greatness?

I settled into the new role and ran it well for about two years. Starting the business and watching it grow had kept me engaged and excited, but after a decade, I didn't love my job anymore. Knowing the company was on the path to greatness didn't leave me feeling fulfilled. Being on the top in a successful company, it turns out, didn't bring me the energy, joy, and satisfaction I thought it might.

Why Goodness over Greatness?

I'll admit, I struggle when I think about people who seek influential positions in order to control rather than influence. They see greatness as the pursuit of excellence, achievement, and success, but in a way that merely gains recognition or admiration. When accomplishments become the foundation of greatness, it often comes at the expense of goodness.

Some might wonder, "What, then, is 'goodness'?"

I believe goodness is a dedication to character and integrity and choices that prioritize the well-being of oneself and others. Goodness is the place where lasting fulfillment, positive impact, and valuing people and principles over personal accolades find grounding.

Greatness has its roots in what you get done, while goodness is based on character. The philosophy of Goodness over Greatness challenges leaders to prioritize principles over prestige. I want to transform the perspective of greatness by placing character ahead of success and achievement without putting them in opposition to one another. This philosophy calls us to create an impact that resonates on a deeper, more lasting level and encourages the achievements of greatness without sacrificing core values.

I like to think of this as leading from the inside out. My approach is no doubt *influenced* by my faith. But the idea certainly is not *limited to* my faith. One of Jesus' least popular topics among the Temple rulers was the notion that the religious leaders of his day needed to clean the inside before they started trying to clean up those around them. And Christianity isn't the only religion or philosophical tradition that embraces the importance of inner character and virtue over outward appearance or displays.

Too many people lead behind a superficial facade. Like the great Wizard of Oz, they don't want anyone to know who they really are. But trying to lead from this "great on the outside" perspective is exhausting. It causes tension, heart-ache, and burnout.

I prefer inside-out leadership, and the key to the process is starting with ME instead of WE. It involves developing the inner character through a mindset shift and self-aware-ness. Reading from this perspective will give you the stron-gest advantage.

Leveraging a Mindset Shift

Everyone has something called "selective attention." We direct our focus to the things we believe are *most relevant* and ignore the information we see as *irrelevant*. For instance, take a minute, stop reading, and count all the blue things around you. Now, write that number in the margin or hold it in your memory.

Did you finish?

Next, without scanning the room, write in the margin the number of *pink* things you remember seeing.

If you're like most, you might recall one or two, especially if you're sitting in your own home, but you likely won't be able to come up with an exact number. Anytime we begin looking specifically for one thing, it becomes most relevant, and we miss everything else—the things our brain deems irrelevant.

It reminds me of the rearview mirror in my new car. Recently, while on vacation, luggage stacked in the back of my SUV blocked my view. I decided this was the perfect excuse to use a new technology feature on my car. I flipped a switch, and the rear-view mirror turned into a digital camera feed, allowing me to see the road behind me.

There's just one problem. Every time I looked up, my eyes had to refocus. My mind expected a mirrored view of the road behind me with a focal distance of five to fifteen feet.

Instead, the digital screen gave me a focal distance of about eighteen inches. This meant for a second, my brain had to figure out what I was looking at and how far away it was. I eventually tried a little experiment. Every time I needed to look in my rear-view mirror, I reminded myself the image would be a screen rather than a mirror. Sure enough, I had instant focus on what was on the screen—no more delay. When I expected a nearby digital screen, my eyes immediately focused correctly.

We can leverage that same mental advantage. If we *expect* to learn, we will. If we *expect* to discover something new, we will. And if we begin to look for the best part of ourselves deep within, we'll find it. It's a powerful and wonderful tool our brain gives us. Your first mental move on this journey of Goodness over Greatness is to *look for and count all the ways you can begin to lead from the inside-out.*

Becoming a strong, impactful leader means aligning your actions with your core principles, embracing who you are, and seeing greatness as valuable only when built upon a foundation of goodness, making it authentic, sustainable, and meaningful.

It's that very mindset shift that set me on a path toward being excited to get out of bed every morning once again. I finally decided I needed to fire myself during a John Maxwell event. Dr. Maxwell said, "Sometimes you have to give up to go up." I knew I needed to give up my position in Focus Lab, so I stepped down from the leadership of the company and started *Built on Purpose*. Though I maintained ownership, I was free to pursue what I believe I was created to be.

I could have continued to be a key leader in a well-respected business, but I'd have been miserable and exhausted. I love executive coaching. Helping entrepreneurs and business leaders find direction in their careers energizes me. It wasn't easy to let go of a company I helped found, but Focus Lab didn't need a full-time coach. Though it took almost fifteen years for me to move into this place where I can be the best possible version of myself, I don't regret a day of the slow shift. I learned a great deal about how to build a business and help others draw their roadmap of goodness.

Getting the Most Out of This Book

Two primary goals drive this book. And though they may sound like opposites at first glance, in true yin and yang fashion, they're actually complementary.

First, I wanted to write a book that could be read quickly. Maybe over a weekend, or for faster readers like my wife, maybe in a single sitting. Second, I wanted a book that required a certain slowness of pace to get the most out of it. After all, like my journey—one that isn't completely finished—inside-out work is often slow.

The following pages will lead you on a journey I take with my clients. Each chapter ends with a few questions. Don't misjudge the brevity. They can bring tremendous value if you sit with them. Don't be afraid to wrestle with them. To get the most from this book, stop and take some time with each question.

John Maxwell often says he reads a good book twice— once to mark the book and a second time to let the book mark him. Even if you initially read this in a single sitting or over a weekend, don't let it stop there. Too often, we read the words and devote little time to acting on what we've read.

Knowledge isn't power. Action is. Knowledge is just a fuel source at rest, waiting to be used.

You've heard the phrase "knowledge is power." I disagree. I believe action is power. Knowledge is just a fuel source at rest, waiting to be used. Give yourself the gift of action as you go. After all, there's no inside-out growth without action.

I have a passion to help others rise to their best selves through inside-out Goodness over Greatness leadership. Since each person has a unique learning style, I've developed a variety of extra resources. At GoodnessOverGreatness.com, you'll find a workbook, inventories, and a series of companion emails you can sign up to receive as you continue through the book. So, check them out as we continue to explore Goodness over Greatness.

CHAPTER ONE

THE HISTORY OF GREATNESS

You were designed for accomplishment,
engineered for success,
and endowed with the seeds of greatness.

—Zig Ziglar

Throughout history, famous men and women have given the world the impression that *good* is a roadblock to *greatness*. John D. Rockefeller said, "Don't be afraid to give up the good to go for the great." And in a book I truly enjoyed, *Good to Great*, Jim Collins writes, "Good is the enemy of great. And that is one of the key reasons why we have so little that becomes great. . . . Few people attain great lives, in large part because it is just so easy to settle for a good life."

But both men talked about good as an adjective, an outer demonstration, rather than the noun or something less visible.

Merriam-Webster defines the adjective as "agreeable, pleasant, attractive, fit, adequate, wholesome, salutary, amusing, or clever." The dictionary defines the noun with phrases that go much deeper: "morally proper, kind, useful, beneficial, honest, genuine, helpful, and of praiseworthy character."[2] Sadly, many believe they have to sacrifice every kind of good to attain greatness. They have a skewed view of what Jim Collins meant. They give up the kind, useful, genuine, praiseworthy parts of their good to move on to greatness and settle for a merely sufficient and satisfactory life.

The Sad Example from Today's Leaders

If we watch the political arena, we might think that sacrificing good on the altar of great is mandatory for success. Many leaders of our country have risen to what some might call greatness, but we see so much back-biting and deceit in that realm that the term "leader" has turned into a negative. Too many politicians and leaders in business have achieved greatness on the back of someone else to whom they gave no credit. Many have trampled and harmed their colleagues and others on the way up the ladder of success. This picture of leadership makes us cringe. In fact, some leaders have left such a bad taste in our mouths, we find it hard to see good in anyone who rises to a high position.

Net worth also seems to set the bar for apparent greatness. Most people believe the more money you have, the more successful you are. John D. Rockefeller was the founder of the Standard Oil Company, the very first billionaire, and at one time the richest man on the entire planet. He started making money as a very young man and traveled the road to "greatness" his entire life. A reporter once asked him, "How much money is enough?" To which he calmly replied, "Just a little bit more."

But isn't that a big component of greatness—a little bit more? No matter how high someone rises on the corporate ladder, they want the next thing. In every aspect of achievement and accomplishment, I see people looking for that "little bit more."

Gamblers often "win big" at least once, but those with the compulsion to win "a little bit more" end up losing everything they won and a good deal of their original investment.

The world holds countless stories of men and women who squandered tens of thousands of dollars trying to get "a little bit more." Some have even pushed so far that they lost their parents' fortunes or their siblings' houses.

Don't Sacrifice Goodness on the Altar of Greatness

I have nothing against greatness as a concept or a goal. In fact, it's something I aspire to myself. However, greatness too often becomes the solitary focus. And when this happens, it comes at great cost. The Vanderbilt family felt the effects firsthand.

Though born into a poor Dutch family, Cornelius Vanderbilt, "Commodore," became a very successful man. Even with limited education, he rose to amass some of the greatest wealth of his time. His fortune could easily have been handed down for generations; however, within four decades of his death, everything Commodore and his son William had built was gone.

Commodore's grandchildren and great-grandchildren squandered every penny. They didn't give it away to worthy charities, and it's not that they were just lazy. They used their wealth to build huge houses and impress the "old-money" crowd. They were driven to have other greats acknowledge their success.

A few sources believe the reason the Vanderbilt fortune went so quickly was Commodore's character. He wasn't kind to his children and didn't teach them a thing about money. He was known as shrewd, aggressive, ruthless, rough, and uncultured. His only two charitable donations came in the form of a steamship given to the North to help with the Civil War efforts and a million dollars he gave to start the university named after him.

Before he died, Commodore's son William was noted to have said:

> I have my house, my pictures, and my horses, and so do they. I can have a steam yacht if I want to, but it would give me no pleasure, and I don't care for it. [My neighbor] isn't worth a hundredth part as much as I am, but he has more of the real pleasures of life than I have. His house is as comfortable as mine, even if it didn't cost so much; his team is about as good as mine; his opera box is next to mine; his health is better than mine, and he will probably outlive me. And he can trust his friends." According to the author of *Fortune's Children*, this second-generation Vanderbilt believed "being the richest person in the world brought him...nothing but anxiety.[3] [4]

The Greatness Traps[IP] That Derail Us

On the Goodness Journey[IP], there are exits that seem worth taking. Promises of recognition, success, and significance lure us off course. But these exits often lead us to places that look impressive from the outside and feel hollow on the inside.

I call them **Greatness Traps**.

They don't always look bad. In fact, they usually look smart, strategic, and even admirable. They promise the very things traditional thinking tells us we need, causing us to believe we should put our energy into becoming successful and making a good living for our family. But the danger is this: the more time we spend in them, the further we drift from what makes us whole. These traps can sabotage our well-being, compromise our values, and ultimately keep us from becoming the person we actually want to be. (See the Appendix for a complete list of these Greatness Traps.)

One of the Greatness Traps that I think the Vanderbilt family fell into is what I call **Saving that Becomes Hoarding**. Amassing such wealth, only to store it away for generational wealth, comes with consequences.

Greatness Traps can sabotage our well-being, compromise our values, and ultimately keep us from becoming the person we actually want to be.

The danger of falling into the Greatness Trap isn't limited to a century ago. In his book *Never Enough*, Andrew Wilkinson shared his own struggle with greatness. In the first chapter, he shares his thoughts during those few weeks prior to reaching the billionaire mark. Looking out from a plane window, he started to wonder how many of the people he watched riding bikes and kayaking below were truly happy. And as they turned into dots below him, he confessed, "In truth, I knew I wasn't [happy], even with all the money I had."[5]

More over Enough is another primary Greatness Trap, characterized by constant upgrading, lack of satisfaction, and always wanting to reach an elusive next level. In Andrew's case, memories of poverty drove him to feel like he needed more. When the wealthy played their "What's your number?" game, Andrew joined. "What number would you need to see in your bank account to feel as though you had enough?" He discovered that no matter how much someone had, it was never enough. "Everyone...irrespective of where they sat in the pecking order of success, answered the question in almost the same way: they would be happy if only they were able to 'double' what they already had. The person with $500,000 in the bank would feel secure when they had $1 million. Someone with $1 million in savings just wanted two."

The billionaire came to appreciate this quote from John D. Rockefeller: "I know of nothing more despicable and pathetic than a man who devotes all the hours of the waking day to the making of money for money's sake."

Don't Settle

I don't want anyone to settle. Helping you live an adequate life is not my goal. I want you to thrive. We should definitely strive for more than "good enough," but at the same time, do you ever get tired of only striving? It's hard work climbing the ladder and beating others to the finish line. More than one person has faced burnout, anxiety, helplessness, and depression because they focused on money and status.

Jim Collins is right, settling for good enough is the enemy of greatness. But what if we're missing out on all the benefits of greatness because we're putting it ahead of goodness? What if this idea of goodness that lies in morality, humility, principle, and giving is actually the foundation of greatness rather than the enemy?

Greatness is about *doing and achieving*. Goodness is about *being*. When greatness becomes an ideal we will sacrifice everything for, it turns into our nemesis. It robs us of our very best life. After all, "What good is it for someone to gain the whole world, yet forfeit their soul?"[6]

Greatness is about *doing and achieving*. Goodness is about *being*.

When we settle for greatness without a complete picture of goodness, we lose ourselves. Greatness will steal our freedom if we let it, sneaking in before we even realize it, especially if we haven't identified our personal definition of success.

CHAPTER TWO

WORKING TOWARD SUCCESS AND GREATNESS

*Defining greatness is perhaps
even harder than achieving it.*

—John Wooden

So, how about it? How do *you* define success?

I love asking this question because it brings a vast spectrum of answers. However, if I rephrase the question, "What do you picture when I say, 'He's an extremely successful man,'" nearly everyone imagines someone in a suit and tie, a professional sports jersey, or at least someone with high net worth. Society uses terms like power couple, corner office, and breaking the glass ceiling. When we start to define the successful person, net worth becomes a major drive in our interpretation.

Most people see success as a list of accolades and achievements. And in many cases, if people were honest with themselves, they would see that success and the achievements that accompany it are closely related to their identity.

Take a moment and list the ways you describe yourself.

_____

_____

_____

_____

How many of the words you used are related to your work? Ask yourself, "If I didn't have my position, how would I feel about myself?" How much of your identity is related to reaching the top of the ladder?

Henri Nouwen presented three lies we tell ourselves when answering the question of identity: I am what I do, I am what others say about me, or I am what I have. These three statements often contain elements of how we see ourselves and our value and undergird our perception of our worth. Nouwen would say, "life often follows a repetitive up-and-down motion" when we think this way.[7] Does your description of yourself fall into any of these three categories?

The Journey of a True Hero

I love a good hero movie. One of the most drastic hero transformations I've ever seen appeared on the big screen as the adopted son of a noodle chef felt pushed to answer the call of greatness. He resisted for a time because deep inside, he didn't want to fight the five who were training for the position. He admired each of his potential competitors. Overweight and out of shape, no one thought the heir to a noodle empire could possibly be the nation's next savior. It didn't take long for the audience to see that the frightened and unskilled Po would need a huge outward transformation if he was ever to become the Dragon Warrior.

Like every true hero, the giant black and white bear the world has come to love as *Kung Fu Panda* went through a double transformation. Yes, he had to learn to be quick on his feet and harness his clumsiness. But more than that, Po had to have a mindset shift and internal metamorphosis so he could see himself as the leader he was created to be. Internally, the big lovable character had to understand that he could maintain his values of family first, non-violence, and accepting those around him while becoming a strong warrior and revered leader. The external transformation without the internal would have netted a second Tai Lung, the leopard who wanted the title of Dragon Warrior so desperately that he would kill for it.

Looking for More

Many of the people I talk to, especially the younger generations, struggle with the thought of success at any cost. Even if they want to rise to the top, they feel a sense of disconnect when they face that picture of external achievement. During their internships and work, they find themselves surrounded by overachievers and people who will do anything for recognition. Compromise looks like the only way to get ahead.

Even though these young people look up to those who've reached great heights—and even aspire to get there someday themselves—something just doesn't sit right. They feel the push to keep moving, work more hours, and make sure the right people see them. But they often aren't energized the same way their bosses or mentors are. The path to greatness they see just doesn't motivate them. Something feels off.

More and more people are growing hungry for something bigger than merely winning.

The shiny perks look impressive, and they pull like a powerful magnet. The thought of power, wealth, and greatness can be irresistible, but the concept also creates an indescribable dissonance within those who have developed a more altruistic view of life.

The chasing and striving appear necessary; however, as these same people gaze inward, they sense there's another way—a better way. I like the notion that more and more people are growing hungry for something bigger than merely winning. But too many haven't figured out how to live up to their potential and make it to the top without compromising their values. How do we discover what's missing?

The Journey of Goodness

I've been blessed with success in my businesses; however, I've noticed that without goodness continually in my sights—an idea we'll explore in the next few chapters—the weight of the world becomes difficult to carry. To stay resilient and strong, I've created a Roadmap for my life that emphasizes goodness and a Rhythm that reinforces it.

It's normal for people to think *doing* specific things will allow them to achieve greatness. In short, they believe "Doing leads to achieving." To their credit, greatness isn't attainable without action. Unfortunately, action without intention is another Greatness Trap. Constant striving doesn't leave time for us to consider what we are *becoming*.

Becoming is a never-ending process that adds richness to your life. It's the key to living in the model of Goodness over Greatness. However, *becoming* requires a mindset shift as well as an awareness of how our actions affect our inner selves and those around us. This flow of attaining and reinforcing goodness has the power to sustain us during the harsh winds of greatness.

The Goodness Journey adds knowledge, insight, and a greater perspective on life that allows us to give back in a productive way and make a huge impact on those around us.

As Lao Tzu said, "Watch your thoughts, they become your words; watch your words, they become your actions; watch your actions, they become your habits; watch your habits, they become your character; watch your character, it becomes your destiny." This is the essence of moving toward a Goodness over Greatness mindset.

Achieving outward success without a healthy start on the Goodness Journey makes it easy to miss the massive intangible benefits that accompany goodness. I don't want anyone to miss those rewards. My deepest desire is for everyone

The Goodness Journey adds knowledge, insight, and a greater perspective on life that allows us to give back in a productive way and make a huge impact on those around us.

I encounter to be able to find success. But I want it to be true success. I don't want you to wake up when you're seventy and discover your life ended up like William Vanderbilt.

When I work privately with one-on-one coaching clients, we use a framework I call The Goodness Journey. The Goodness Journey helps people move from a life of striving to a world of thriving. This approach and process has helped individuals uncover their deepest **Reasons** for walking their chosen path. It then shows us how to define our current **Reality**. With our present and future described, we can then draw a **Roadmap** to walk while we create a **Rhythm** of progress as we travel. And for those who find themselves stuck along the way, this process

The 4 Rs on the Goodness Journey
Reasons
Reality
Roadmap
Rhythm

might need a fifth R. Even the most able-bodied sometimes need a season of **Rescue** so they can get started on their journey.

I know many people would prefer to have easy-to-follow, step-by-step instructions; however, like any road trip, the routes we travel on the Goodness Journey often have detours and roadblocks. We might have to circle back, and each overlap we encounter will require perseverance, but this just makes the journey an adventure.

The beautiful thing about this process is that it is cyclical and exponential and offers limitless potential for growth. Even before you reach the end of the first loop, you begin to strengthen your foundation, and each time you complete a circle, you discover you've taken your character to a higher level and expanded your influence and impact.

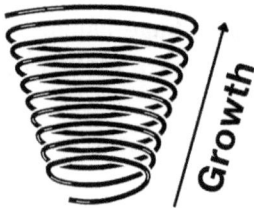

However, as you already know, the only way to start any trip is to take the first step. You can read and absorb, but without movement, we can't really call it a journey. Po would never have become Dragon Warrior without the long, arduous climb up the mountain. So, let's turn the page and take the first step toward Goodness over Greatness.

CHAPTER THREE

WHAT DO YOU WANT TO BE WHEN YOU GROW UP

We cannot become
what we need to be
by remaining what we are.
—Max De Pree

Grown-ups have a standard question for young people. We reword it depending on the age, but the intent remains the same. When we talk to high school students, we say something like, "What are your plans after college?" You might ask middle schoolers, "Have you started thinking about what job you want to do when you get older?" But elementary children hear the root question, "What do you want to be when you grow up?"

Every answer will be different, but all include achievement and aspirations. Kindergartners want to be firemen and doctors, nurses and gamers. Even football players and musicians make the list. Sadly, this achievement-based question leaves out an important part of the goodness equation.

What Shapes Your Picture of Greatness

Humans seem to have this need to be better than everyone else. Early civilizations went to war over who would be king

13

and which country owned the most land. Power and authority have been sought after for millennia. These days, we have daily debates to pinpoint the GOAT—the Greatest of All Time—in various areas of culture. The quest for greatness isn't new.

After all, success, wealth, and power seem to have walked hand-in-hand for centuries. Nearly two hundred years ago, Alexander Hamilton said, "A fondness for power is implanted in most men, and it is natural to abuse it when acquired."[8]

Before we can take the first step in this journey of Goodness over Greatness, we need to consider what shapes our particular view of greatness. Some look to their parents or educators for the definition. These important people in our lives just want us to be the best we can be. They push us to make ourselves "a little bit better."

Others base their idea of success on what they see on television or social media. How many followers does a person have? Are they considered an influencer? Watch the way children change their clothing styles or music preferences. These small, seemingly inconsequential things speak volumes about their idea of success.

Sadly, many people have themselves boxed into a particular path to greatness. Some have allowed others to do it for them. They believe the hype and don't see any other way to "the top." Others feel trapped in mediocrity because they have been convinced success is limited to unethical, high-net-worth crooks, and they can't live that way.

The problem we face in defining success lies in a lesson we can learn from the movie *Captain America: The First Avenger*. I recently enjoyed watching the Marvel movie with my teen and pre-teen. When the scrawny Steve Rogers walked into the experimental government lab, I started to see the parallel to Goodness over Greatness. Steve Rogers desperately wanted to serve his country, but he wasn't a prime candidate for combat because of his size, poor health, and demeanor.

Scientist Abraham Erksine had discovered a secret serum with the potential to transform even the weakest individual into a person with superhuman strength. Erksine had seen its power when a Nazi scientist, Johann Schmidt, took the first injection. Schmidt believed he had risen to supreme greatness, but Erksine knew the experiment needed someone of the highest moral character.

When Rogers asked him, "Why me?" Abraham Erksine explained the project to the Captain, "The serum amplifies everything that is inside, so good becomes great; bad becomes worse. This is why you were chosen. Because the strong man who has known power all his life may lose respect for that power, but a weak man knows the value of strength, and knows... compassion." He goes on to say, "Whatever happens tomorrow, you must promise me one thing. That you will stay who you are, not a perfect soldier, but a good man."[9]

Redefining Success

Success, wealth, and power are the serum that reveals what is truly inside a person. They amplify the good or bad—the constructive or destructive nature within. Unfortunately, the world tends to focus on what I call Destructive Success[IP]. This kind of victory often makes the headlines in a not-so-positive way.

Enron cornered the market on natural gas contracts in the 1980s. Their staff, a bunch of innovative, creative decision makers, were sometimes called the smartest guys in the room. But when things started going downhill, they employed sketchy tactics to hide their failing profit margin. When documents began to be shredded after reports of a decrease in shareholder equity of $1.2 billion, the SEC stepped in. Within a few years of their bankruptcy, many of Enron's most successful executives found themselves in prison.[10]

General Electric was once the premier business name in America. Everyone had some sort of GE appliance. They made light bulbs, x-ray machines, toaster ovens, and more available to the public. They actually boasted about their significant salaries. In fact, they told the world how much they paid in taxes because they wanted to contribute to the growth of the United States. Then, in 1981, they hired Jack Welch to lead the company.

For the next twenty years, GE became known for cost-cutting and quarterly earnings at the hands of a ruthless executive. In his first few years at the helm, Welch got rid of about 100,000 employees and closed many factories. He paved the way for outsourcing to other countries, and mid-way through his tenure, the company hit the number one spot on the stock exchange.

Welch's successor picked up where he left off, and within twenty years, GE was sold off to several other companies. The most successful company in America fell to legal but savage business strategies—tactics that many other companies picked up on because they saw the short-term gains they created.[11] Companies profit by cutting ten percent of their staff every year and being cutthroat in their dealings, but they end up self-destructing.

That is Destructive Success. But on the opposite side of the spectrum, we have Constructive Success[IP].

One of the most positive things to come from Jack Welch's questionable business deals was the introduction of Conscious Capitalism. John Mackey and Raj Sisodia coined the term in their book *Conscious Capitalism: Liberating the Heroic Spirit of Business*. This former CEO of Whole Foods, along with his marketing professor friend, suggested that businesses should look for more ethical and equitable ways to get things done. They forged the phrase from a quote by Nobel Prize Winner Muhammad Yunus. Yunus wanted to build a bank in Bangladesh that was a "socially conscious capitalist enterprise." Mackey and Sisodia call Conscious Capitalism "human, vibrant, and one of the most powerful tools for creating a better society."[12]

As I mentioned before, I don't believe there's anything wrong with success. In fact, greatness and success give us a host of opportunities to make this world a better place. The key is choosing which kind of success you want, then doing something to achieve it.

Building a Strong Foundation

Steve Rogers had more success than Johann Schmidt when he took the serum injection because deep within, he had the characteristics that make for a strong foundation. One of the reasons we love a good movie is the fact that we enjoy seeing the good guy win. When we root for the underdog, it's not because he needs a cheering section. We want him to win because we can see his character strengths. We resonate with his honesty and integrity. Even if the guy was a scoundrel for a time, we love seeing him turn over a new leaf.

In the late 1700s, Edmund Burke said, "The greater the power, the more dangerous the abuse." And we've all seen this play out at our workplace and in politics. Like Captain America's serum, power, wealth, and influence won't make you better or worse; they will simply reveal the true character within.

What Do You Want to Be *Like* When You Grow Up?[IP]

We all have traits we're born with; however, character doesn't fall in that category. We each get to choose what kind of person we want to be. To build character, we need to add just one simple word to our original question. Instead of asking,

"What do you want to be when you grow up?" we should ask, "What do you want to be LIKE when you grow up?" When you begin to answer this second question, you find that many of the things you would have used as answers to the root question don't fit.

What do you want to be LIKE when you grow up?

"I want to be successful" doesn't work when you convert it to "I want to be like successful."

"I want to be a football player" falls short as "I want to be like a football player."

However, you could very well say, "I want to be like my grandfather." This allows you to dig even deeper. The question then becomes, "What qualities did he have that you want to emulate?" Perhaps Grandpa was kind and tough, full of joy, firm, honest, or hard-working. With a bit of intentionality, you can build a character just like grandpa, grandma, your favorite teacher, or a mixture of all the people you admire.

Many of us can articulate our outward journey. We know where we want to end up in our career or skill set. We have travel plans and bucket lists. It's easy to define what we want to achieve, but how do you tell people *who you want to become* to reach your goals?

In all our favorite superhero movies, we see a guide or sensei leading the pupil. Our hero has lessons to learn, and we see the growth as they put the lessons to work in their lives. Every level of change requires choices; these men and women display intentionality as they implement the teaching of their elders.

Inside-out growth demands this same kind of intentionality. We can't simply want to be better, more courageous, or more vocal. We have to choose to make the moves that will catapult our growth.

As we delve into this five-step process, focus on defining what you want to be like at the end of the journey. The more clarity you have, the greater likelihood you have of reaching your destination. We may make a few unexpected turns along the way as we refine **Inside-out growth demands intentionality. We have to choose to make the moves that will catapult our growth.** our goals and put our character into specific situations. I think one of the most exciting things about this adventure is that we never really arrive. We just keep growing, rising, and expanding. Just like the serum enhanced the strongest qualities in Johann Schmidt and Steve Rogers, these five steps have the power to strengthen and deepen your most prominent characteristics.

Constructive Success begins with character. It occurs when we focus on what is true, noble, right, pure, lovely, admirable, and praiseworthy.[13] But before we move on, take a few moments and answer this tough question: What do you want to be LIKE when you grow up?

_____

_____

_____

_____

_____

CHAPTER FOUR

IDENTIFY YOUR REASONS

There is no greatness
where there is no simplicity, goodness and truth.
—Leo Tolstoy

Few get in a car without a destination in mind. Every pilot and ship's captain knows exactly where they plan to disembark. Even if a storm forces them to reroute, the purpose in their mission doesn't change. Answering the question of what you want to be LIKE when you grow up will set the stage as you begin to identify your destination.

The Goodness Journey begins with identifying your Reasons. Laying this foundation for our goals and aspirations equips us to do our jobs better and allows us to truly lead from the inside out.

Determining your Reasons might prove as challenging as deciding where to go on your next big vacation. Many entrepreneurs and leaders have a variety of talents and interests, and the possibilities might all sound intriguing. To assist the people I work with, I've come up with some tools to help them discover their whys. If we don't take time to understand what drives us, we could easily fall into routines and embrace expectations created by others. The right questions can give us clarity and increase the resolution of the photo of our future.

Your Core Values Lay the Foundation for Your Reasons

Let's start with the question, "What do I value most?"

Today, we hear many leaders talk about core values. Maybe you thought this concept was limited to businesses. Truthfully, though, everyone has a set of characteristics they find most important and a collection of fundamentals they won't compromise on. Sadly, not everyone has taken the time to define their personal core values. If we neglect to identify these things that are most significant to us, we become susceptible to doing things and accepting responsibilities that don't align with our beliefs.

If you already have a set of core values for your business, it will be tempting to skip this first exercise. But that would be a mistake. Even if your company's core values flowed through you in some fashion, you will probably find some distinctions in your personal core values.

> **Everyone has a set of characteristics they find most important and a collection of fundamentals they won't compromise on.**

Here's where we get to work. I have a list of one hundred potential characteristics, relationships, and beliefs most people include in their personal lists. It includes things like family, integrity, self-respect, status, and wisdom. I included the full list in the free resources at GoodnessOverGreatness.com. Go grab that list as we move through this section of the book.

As you reference this roster of words with their definitions, work through them slowly. Consider printing them so you can circle the ones you resonate with most. Don't worry about narrowing it down. Anything that makes you say, "Yes, that's important to me," qualifies.

Next, take about ten minutes to narrow down your list to the top twenty to twenty-five. Ask yourself, "Is this value essential to who I am?" and "Would I feel a sense of loss or discomfort if this value were absent from my life?" Eliminate any values that you don't answer yes to.

We're not done yet. Next, it's time to cut your value list in half by asking, "Does this value represent a deep part of who I am?" or "How often does this value influence my choices or actions?" You might also look through the list for similar words. For example, if you've chosen both friendship and relationships, you might choose one of the two to represent both.

From this list, we're going to choose our five core values. Don't rush this part. Look for the five words that feel most foundational to you. Which values best reflect what you want to prioritize? Which values guide your decision-making and bring a sense of fulfillment? Which ones will best help you reach your destination?

Take at least fifteen minutes to select and write your final core values below and create your own definition for each one. What does the word mean to you for your life? How does it resonate with you? Then describe why this is important to you.

Value 1 _____

Means to me:

_____

Important to me because:

_____

Value 2 _____

Means to me:

_____

Important to me because:

_____

Value 3 _____

Means to me:

_____

Important to me because:

_____

Value 4 _____

Means to me:

_____

Important to me because:

_____

Value 5 _____

Means to me:

_____

Important to me because:

_____

The Inside-Out Wheel[IP]

The Inside-Out Wheel can also be a useful tool to help you bring your future into focus. You'll find similar tools across the internet. The goal of this exercise is to choose the areas of your life you believe are most important. Step one: Pick six to eight things from this or modify it as it fits your life best. Take out the areas that don't resonate and add things that are more important to your well-being.

Money and Finance

1   2   3   4   5   6   7   8   9   10

Career and Work

1   2   3   4   5   6   7   8   9   10

Health and Fitness

1   2   3   4   5   6   7   8   9   10

Fun and Recreation

1   2   3   4   5   6   7   8   9   10

Environmental

1   2   3   4   5   6   7   8   9   10

Community Involvement

1   2   3   4   5   6   7   8   9   10

Friends and Family

1   2   3   4   5   6   7   8   9   10

Partner and Love

1   2   3   4   5   6   7   8   9   10

Growth and Learning

1   2   3   4   5   6   7   8   9   10

Faith and Spirituality

1   2   3   4   5   6   7   8   9   10

Step two: Rate each on a scale of one to ten based on how satisfied you are with that area of your life, one being not at all satisfied, ten being highly satisfied. After you circle the number that most closely reflects your satisfaction level, write your personal eight areas of satisfaction in the outer ring of the Inside-Out Wheel below.

Inside-Out Wheel

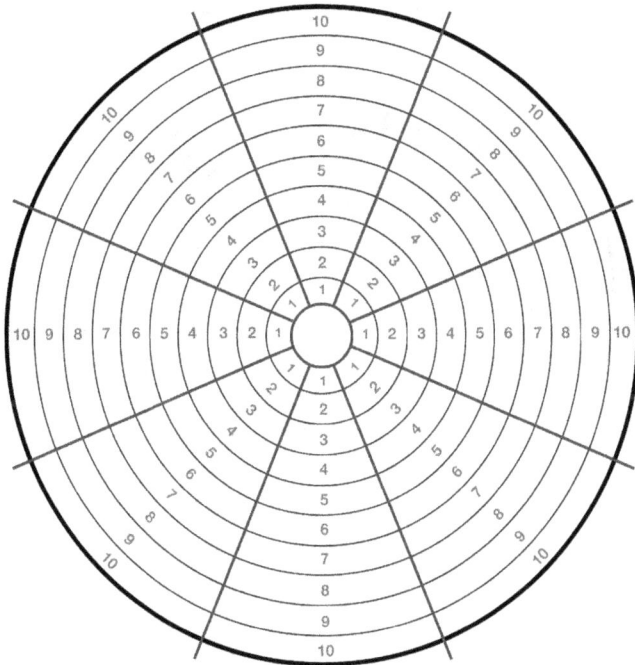

Then fill in the number on the wheel that corresponds to the number you assigned that area. Finally, draw lines to create a continuous connection between sections. How closely does your line resemble a circle? Don't worry if it's not a perfectly round shape. High satisfaction will be more important to you in some areas than others. However, it gives you a snapshot of your life in the moment and can help you identify the Reasons for your actions. It will probably look different next week, and it could change drastically over a year or more. Your main task is to determine how you want to change the inner shape you created. Which areas draw your attention? Why does it need your attention? What would it take to increase your level of satisfaction in that area?

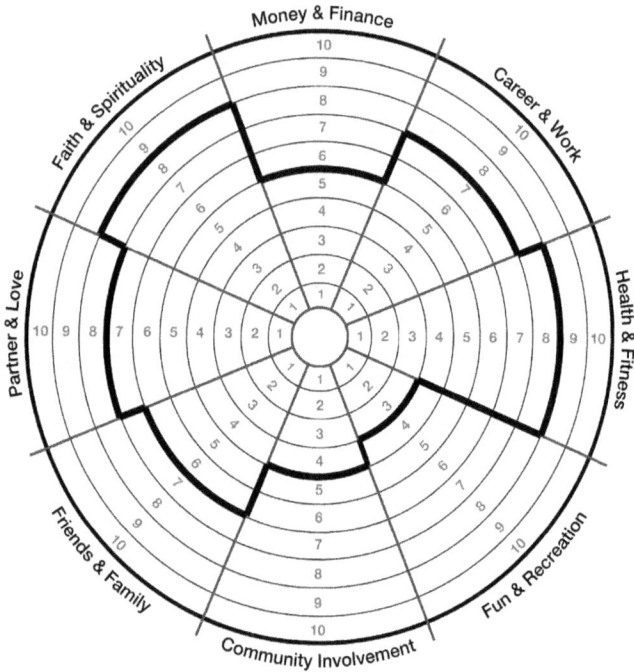

This is a completed Inside-Out Wheel to give you an idea of what your Wheel could potentially look like.

Repeat this exercise once a month or once a quarter for the first year and then as often as you feel like the areas of your life aren't quite as balanced as you like. You can find a fillable template in the resources available at GoodnessOverGreatness.com.

Asking the Right Questions

Finally, I've developed a few questions you can ask yourself to bring your current world more into focus and identify your Reasons. First, consider the things in your life that excite you:

- Which parts of my personal life give me energy?
- What work goals electrify me?

Describe in detail the parts that bring you the most delight. As you dig deep into the most intriguing areas of your goals, you'll begin to unearth the things that feed the purpose of your life. You may have the same goal as several people on your team, yet the part of the goal that fulfills each of you could be completely different.

Next, go even deeper:

- What will be different for me if I accomplish this goal?
- What will I gain?

You might come up with a variety of answers to those questions; however, take a minute to focus on the first or second that comes to your mind. Those are the ones that will increase your clarity.

As you finish, ask one more important question:

- If I achieve this goal, how will it impact those around me?

This includes family, friends, coworkers, colleagues, and anyone else your life touches on a regular basis. The impact may be positive, negative, or neutral. Our lives constantly touch others, so everything we do has a ripple effect. It's important to consider how far the ripples will extend. And how far we *want them* to extend. This doesn't mean we have to abandon goals because of the way they impact others. However, without taking that into consideration, our success has the potential to become Destructive rather than Constructive. We may become great in the eyes of the media, but will it be good?

Some early-stage entrepreneurs I coach identify reaching a million dollars in their business as the thing that excites them most. But when they dig deeper, we demonstrate how common it is to reevaluate our destination. When we peel that million-dollar goal back a bit, these entrepreneurs experience a change of focus.

"What will be different when you have a million-dollar-plus business? What will you gain?" I ask.

"I'll be able to say I have a million-dollar business."

You can almost see their surprise as they realize their answer stole some of their excitement.

"Wait, is that really the only thing that will change? I'm not so sure that will make enough difference to be worthwhile," they continue. "Now that I think about it, maybe that's not what my goal should be."

"What else might you want to aim for?" I ask.

"Maybe I should just aim for $500,000 of profit."

"What would be different if you have that kind of profit?"

"Well, that's easy. If I had $500,000, I would pay off my house that year. Oh man, that would be one less thing for me to worry about." Relief covers their face.

Sometimes we go through layers and layers, but often we'll cross into aha moments quickly as the person starts to see their Reasons defined in **What would be different if...** high resolution. I think that's one of the great values of a coach. It's helpful to have someone ask questions that invite you to explore your depths while they listen to your answer and reflect it back to you. Hearing your ideas and solutions from a different perspective can move us into understanding our reasons faster than we could alone.

Before you move forward, take the steps to begin to define your Reasons. Don't get hung up on the things you don't know yet. Many people love low-resolution games like Minecraft®, and others cherish old photocopies made by their grandparents years ago. In the same way, your pixelated Reasons can still be full of joy, fun, and altruism. The resolution doesn't dictate the beauty you can experience in life while you're increasing your clarity.

If you didn't fill in those blanks above, take some time and do that now. Additionally, use the questions below to start a self-guided tour in search of your reasons, or invite a coach to help you leverage your answers and speed up the process.

1. What goals would you like to reach in the next twelve months? What excites you about each one? What will be different if you achieve the goal? What will you gain?

_____

_____

_____

_____

_____

2. Who will these goals impact and how?

_____

_____

_____

_____

_____

CHAPTER FIVE

DEFINE YOUR REALITY

Since we cannot change reality,
let us change the eyes which see reality.
—Nikos Kazantzakis

Every GPS app offers multiple routes to your destination. One will be the shortest distance, and the other will be the fastest route. Some boast no tolls, while others keep you off the highways so you have a more scenic journey. The reality of your choice will depend on the reason for your trip.

The Goodness Journey works the same way. Now that you have your Reasons, it's time to become fully aware of your current Reality. Before moving toward your ultimate goal, it's helpful to take stock of where you are, what resources are at your disposal, and more. By taking an honest look at where we are right now, we can more accurately map the route we should take. Sometimes we can do that alone, while other times we benefit from a thinking partner for this process.

By taking an honest look at where we are right now, we can more accurately map the route we should take.

As I will explain in the next chapter, one of my strengths is finding perspective. In real-life situations, this means I don't mind questions with no definite answers; ambiguity doesn't bother me a bit. For those who prefer clear-cut lines and questionnaires with multiple-choice answers, this method of exploring Reality might feel elusive. However, the most effective leaders dig for the answers to some of the toughest questions you might ever encounter.

Those who like definitive, black-and-white solutions might be troubled by the fluid nature of defining Reality. Roadblocks, detours, and the people we meet along the way force us to return to these questions on a regular basis to make certain our Reality hasn't shifted. Each time you find yourself drifting from your plan or feeling a little lost, come back to these questions and explore them with curiosity and excitement.

What Do I Want?

As we pursue our Reality, the first question we must ask is, "What do I want?" Sometimes this can be difficult to figure out because even those who believe they have a really clear answer often falter after they say it out loud. Suddenly, they realize what they thought they wanted is really what a parent wanted for them, or their desire stems from something they enjoyed in high school. I've seen this happen in many coaching sessions.

Additionally, in many cases, what a person wants changes as they mature. "Before I had kids, I wanted . . ." "When I was twenty, I wanted . . ." While it seems straightforward, answering the "What do I want?" question can be much more complicated than you might think. So, it's important to take some time to allow the answer to develop.

In my case, before I started my first business, I was on a path to be a rock star. Ok, maybe not very far along down that path, but I definitely loved the idea of it. I enjoyed music, particularly playing the guitar and singing, so I could see myself as the next John Mayer or James Taylor. However, as I learned more about what it took to succeed in that field,

I pretty quickly realized it wasn't the life I wanted to pursue or build.

I discovered I wanted to be an entrepreneur almost by accident. While doing some freelancing, I got this itch to build a business and be self-employed. I eventually met my co-founder, and we worked together for a couple of years while keeping our day jobs. We eventually made enough money to feed our families and keep the lights on, so we went full-time into self-employment. Shortly after, we had so much client demand that we realized we needed help.

My reality had changed, and with it my wants. Now I wanted to build a team. For nearly fifteen years now, we've built our business and added people to our organization so we can serve our clients even better.

What Don't I Want?

Experience and maturity give us an excellent view into reality. Time gives us the luxury of asking, "What *don't* I want?"

Someone once asked Michelangelo, "How did you create the statue of David?" He famously replied, "It's simple. I just removed everything that is not David." The great artist knew what he wanted, but the answer to the beauty of the statue was in what he didn't want. For many people, this question of what we don't want is easier to answer than trying to figure out what we do want. And as with Michelangelo's David, the answer often defines a beautiful reality.

When I began exploring that premise of what I don't want after more than a decade of building a team, I realized I didn't want to manage people. I didn't want to lead projects, and I didn't want to be involved in the administration or daily operations of the business any longer. All this reflection forced me to ask how this changed the reality of what I do want. Like Michelangelo, as I chipped away at what I didn't want in my life, I gained clarity into what I wanted the business I run now to be.

Often, listing the things you don't want will roll off your tongue easier than those you do want. Better yet, this list has the potential to bring great clarity. To lead from the inside out, we need this kind of self-awareness.

Despite the fact that age and experience are the greatest factors in answering this question, some younger leaders also know what they don't want because they've watched the adults around them. They've seen their parents and grandparents work too much or watched them miss out on things. My father highly influenced the way I run my business.

My dad had a day job, and he always had side jobs to make sure his family was well cared for. He was a tremendous provider, but I felt like he was always working. So, when I started my first business as a twenty-four-year-old, though I was clueless about being an entrepreneur and couldn't create my list of what I wanted, I knew I didn't want a business that required me to work all the time. Especially given that I was already married with a young daughter.

Understanding what you don't want gives you a greater sense of what you do want. And if you find that you've started your list with things you *don't* want, it's important to make sure you move into identifying the things that you *do* want. It also allows you to include others in your future plans. Do you have a stewardship or volunteer mindset? Would you like to encourage others or give back to the community with your time? What do you want for your children, your spouse, or your grandchildren?

Give Yourself Permission

Maybe you're reading this and thinking, "I don't know what I want. In fact, I'm not even sure I know what I don't want."

You're not alone. Many people in their fifties and sixties still haven't fully defined their reality. Harry Bernstein became a famous author after his ninety-sixth birthday. Gladys Burrill set the World Record for the oldest woman to finish a marathon when she was ninety-two. Peter Roget wrote the famous thesaurus at seventy-three, and the *Little House* series was sixty-five-year-old Laura Ingalls Wilder's first publication.

Some who question their future get stalled. "Since I don't know what I want to do, I won't do anything until I figure it out." Those folks miss out on the opportunities and experiences that will mold them. They skip the things that will help define their reality. How will you discover what you don't want to do if you never do the things you don't want to do?

Give yourself permission to try things that interest you and move on when you discover that particular endeavor doesn't fit your strengths. Think of each of those interests as pixels in a low-resolution photo of your reality. The more things you try, the greater the clarity, and the closer you get to what you want to do, the higher the resolution.

Give yourself permission to try things that interest you and move on when you discover that particular endeavor doesn't fit your strengths.

Defining your reality is all about refining the picture. You may change course a dozen times or more before you figure it out. But each time you use your strengths to create and explore, you march toward that high-resolution picture.

We don't live in our grandparents' culture anymore. Yes, fifty or sixty years ago, when a person started a job, they anticipated retiring from that same company. And a handful of people today may live that reality even today. But at some point over the last six decades, a group of people started to realize, "This doesn't feel right. How can anyone live this way?"

These pioneers paved the way for you and me. When what we're doing doesn't feel right, we can start to ask, "What am I doing in this role or business that I want to keep doing, and what do I not want to do when I make a change?" With each shift in direction, evaluate the things you've learned about yourself. Trust your instincts and use the knowledge you've gained to refine your picture.

Sometimes You Have to Call the Rescue Squad

If you find yourself immobilized at the thought of identifying your Reasons and defining your Reality, you might need to be Rescued. Some people feel like they just don't have time for coaching. They feel so stretched that time for personal development is out of the question.

Even the strongest leaders can get hung up on what I call The 3 Primary Problems[IP]: People Problems, Positioning Problems, or Profitability Problems. When these roadblocks keep someone from enjoying the journey, most often they need to have a conversation with someone skilled in asking the right questions and listening closely.

Much like a pitcher in a slump or musicians who lose the ability to pour themselves into their songs, business leaders who feel stuck probably need a coach to help pull them out of the mire that bogs them down. The value of a coach as you begin to create a Roadmap for your journey can't be overstated, especially if you need someone who can tell the difference between a slow start and being stuck on the starting block.

Begin to Define Your Reality

1. Make two lists: what you want to do and what you don't want to do.

   What I Want to Do   What I Don't Want to Do

   _____   _____

   _____   _____

   _____   _____

   _____   _____

   _____   _____

2. These two lists create a low-resolution picture of your reality. What job could you create for yourself that might explore your interests and incorporate those lists above?

   _____

   _____

   _____

   _____

CHAPTER SIX

THE REALITY OF
YOUR STRENGTHS

The first job of a leader is to define reality.
—Max De Pree

A major step toward understanding your Reality lies in identifying your strengths. In 2001, Gallup® compiled data from several studies and found that only twenty percent of the population works in the areas of their greatest strengths. Sadly, if that's the case, most of us are missing out on being eight times more productive, six times more engaged with our work, and having a quality of life three times better than the rest of the world.[14] Why would we deny ourselves those advantages?

No one wants to come up short, but that's what happens when we ignore our strengths and the strengths of others. Today's high-caliber leaders must develop an awareness of the Reality of what each person does best and use that knowledge to encourage them.

Too many business leaders put employees in the company's most needed positions instead of the place where they can capitalize on their team members' greatest strengths. Often, the employee will have the ability to complete the required tasks efficiently. But, if Gallup is correct, and we can be eight times more productive working within our strengths, businesses could be compromising their bottom line by up to eight hundred percent by implementing that hiring strategy.

With such a small percentage of employees working in the area of their greatest strengths, it's no wonder so many dislike their job and feel unfulfilled, depressed, and anxious. It also explains why some resort to questionable means to climb the ladder. They think they see freedom at the top; however, when achievement becomes our reason rather than the things deep inside that make us tick, we'll never be free.

Unfortunately, sometimes we find it difficult to really understand our strengths. Some people, especially business leaders, can learn almost anything. Many amazing parents expose their children to a variety of mental and physical challenges at a young age, allowing them to adapt to every situation and learn new skills quickly. However, if we've never taken the time to discover which skills relate to our inner being and which ones we developed out of necessity or because it was fun for a short while, we'll eventually burn out. Just because you *can* do everything doesn't mean you *should* do everything.

With such a small percentage of employees working in the area of their greatest strengths, it's no wonder so many dislike their job and feel unfulfilled, depressed, and anxious.

For many years, I did everything rather than delegate. I found myself falling into one of the Greatness Traps. I was afraid others wouldn't get things done the way I did them or do them as well. But no one can sustain growth without help. Dan Sullivan, co-founder and president of Strategic Coach®, believes if we give up the tasks that don't directly align with our strengths to people who can do them at least eighty percent as well as we can, we can increase productivity and save ourselves from burnout.[15] His 80% Approach® has helped many entrepreneurs grow and expand.

The question is, how do we figure out what to delegate? What strengths should we lean into more intentionally? Thankfully, there are some great tools out there that can help.

Leveraging Assessments

The world of self-assessment tools grows larger every year. It can be hard to discern which tests are worth the time, effort, and, sometimes, the cost. And how do you know if they'll actually be valuable over time?

I encourage my clients to take assessments that are high-impact, straightforward to leverage into growth opportunities, and easy to remember. GoodnessOverGreatness. com has links to the ones I recommend. Each reveals a piece of who you are and gives you the information you need to reach the high level of productivity and life enjoyment that Gallup uncovered.

The first assessment I recommend is VIA Character. This assessment has twenty-five years of research behind it. The creators did an international study to see if there were any character traits that were considered a virtue or valued across all cultures. They poured a lot of money into this research and discovered twenty-four character strengths common to every culture. VIA Character has created a free survey that reveals which of these twenty-four traits are most innate to the way you were designed.

The beauty of this assessment is that it allows you to know yourself better. Other equally valid assessments, such as CliftonStrengths® by Gallup, have been created to help you understand how to get more work done by focusing on your innate gifts. This test invites you to discover the things inside you that give you feelings of fulfillment and joy. When you understand your character strengths, you can build stronger relationships, improve your health, overcome challenges, and achieve your goals.

The VIA Character assessment ranks all twenty-four character strengths based on my answers. Seeing them in a list that describes me in detail lets me know which traits might need a bit more effort on my part when others count on me to bring those to the table. We call the top five Signature Strengths. Here are mine for reference:

Perspective   Being able to provide wise counsel to others; having ways of looking at the world that make sense to oneself/others.

Humility   Letting one's accomplishments speak for themselves; not regarding oneself as more special than one is.

Forgiveness   Forgiving those who have done wrong; accepting others' shortcomings; giving people a second chance; not being vengeful.

Fairness   Treating all people the same according to notions of fairness and justice; not letting feelings bias decisions about others; giving everyone a fair chance.

Gratitude   Being aware of and thankful for the good things that happen; taking time to express thanks.

As I go over the top five in the list, I ask myself, "What does it look like to use this strength? How can I leverage Forgiveness or Perspective?" The key to harnessing these strengths is to find a coach or facilitator to dive deep with you to make the most of your best qualities in every situation. This inward-focused assessment is a great setup for the next two because the more you understand yourself, the better you can work and communicate with a team. Take a minute and visit the resources at GoodnessOverGreatness.com to find the link and take your assessment today. Then record your results below.

VIA Character Top Five Results:

1. _____
2. _____
3. _____
4. _____
5. _____

What does it look like to use each of these strengths?

_____

_____

_____

_____

How can I leverage my top two strengths?

_____

_____

_____

Working Genius®

The next assessment I recommend to clients is Working Genius® by Patrick Lencioni. Created to help build healthier and more effective teams, it's also an excellent resource to let you know yourself better. Often, we're thrown into positions and situations that drain us. This can make us feel like a failure or a burden. But what if that's because we're not at the right place in the process?

Working Genius uses a simple acronym, WIDGET, to describe the six primary phases of any project, then asks questions to help us understand which phases bring us the most energy and joy and which are most likely to drain us. The phases in order are Wonder, Invention, Discernment, Galvanizing, Enablement, and Tenacity.

Some people bring a genius of Wonder to the table. They ask questions and look at things from new angles, identifying potential areas for improvement or change. Those with the genius of Invention find energy and joy when they create potential solutions or answers to the posed questions. Discernment is the genius used when assessing the merit and workability of the idea, while those who have the Galvanizing genius generate enthusiasm around the idea. And those who excel in Enablement make sure those with the Genius of Tenacity have all the tools and encouragement they need to bring the project across the finish line.

Understanding your Working Genius can help you understand why you get frustrated or tired while you're working. This assessment also allows you to see how you give to and collaborate with those around you and the way others feed your genius. When we understand the natural flow from Wonder to Invention to Discernment to Galvanizing to Enablement to Tenacity and focus our work in the area of our greatest genius, we find more joy and fulfillment.

Our culture seems to celebrate the Enablement and Tenacity (E-T) folks more than the rest of the team. We live in a goal-oriented culture that often doesn't see or acknowledge those who plan and perfect the project before the hands-on team gets the job done. Some who don't understand the need for the full WIDGET team think the Wonder group just has their heads in the clouds all the time. The Enablement and Tenacity people wish the Wonderers would just stop asking questions that slow them down and try to figure out why the Invention people keep throwing new ideas at them.

Teams that don't understand Working Genius don't label these areas of giftedness like that. Those who naturally bring the project to fruition get frustrated when it takes too long to get the plan to their inbox. At the same time, the people who naturally want every step of the project hashed out and perfected feel pulled when the doers just want to get it done.

The Working Genius model breaks the six phases of work into pairs when you take the assessment. A simple ten-minute assessment will let you see a ranked order of the six stages from the ones that drain you the most to the ones that bring you the most energy. The two that bring you the most energy and fulfillment are called your Geniuses. The two that drain you the most are your Frustrations. And the two in the middle of your ranked results receive the label Competencies. What does all that mean?

Your top two areas, your Geniuses, bring you energy each time you work in them. You probably feel like you could do that type of work all day with no end and still feel great. For example, my areas of Working Genius are Discernment and Wonder. The assessment gave me the title of Contemplative Counselor. This means I get energy and joy from pondering potential, asking "what ifs" and "why nots," and noticing relevant details that many would miss.

I've even noticed that when I attend social gatherings or small groups, and we start to talk about our days, many in the group begin to feel sorry for me (or at least can't relate to me in this way) because if I had a six or seven hours of coaching sessions, I'll say I was "in meetings" all day. They don't realize my areas of Working Genius mean I get energized with those one-on-one meetings that allow me to ask open-ended questions and put things in perspective. Likewise, when you spend time in your areas of Working Genius, you feel more energized and fulfilled.

My Competencies are Invention and Galvanizing. So, I don't mind creating original ideas and solutions, and I can even take those pieces and help put them into a working plan. And my Frustrations are Enablement and Tenacity. This means when I have to get into the nitty gritty of gathering all the details and taking the project across the finish line, I will feel drained pretty quickly.

Keep in mind, this tool doesn't explicitly tell you if you're good or bad at certain things. Its emphasis is on what drains you and energizes you. Because humans have been created to be extremely adaptable, if we work in our areas of competency and frustration long enough, we can often become very good at those phases of project creation. This means we might be tricked into thinking those are our strengths in the Working Genius context. Sadly, if we stay in those positions, even if our performance levels exceed others around us, we're likely to eventually crash and burn.

As an entrepreneur, I spent years taking projects across the finish line. It had to be done, right? At the time, I wasn't aware of the way those final two phases of projects drained me. Without the self-awareness I've discovered since taking this assessment, I felt obligated to carry everything through to completion.

I knew that on the days I had certain meetings and was able to brainstorm, I felt energized when I got home. And I could have told you that during those times, I had to get into the weeds of finishing a project, my family got the exhausted version of me. But I had no idea why. Truthfully, I felt lazy when I knew I needed to get stuff finished. I just didn't want to do it. Not only did I start to feel burned out, but I reached the point where I didn't like my job or my business. Working Genius gave me permission, as well as the language, to not feel lazy. Now I can simply embrace my skills and abilities and design my business in such a way that every person on my team, including me, can leave work energized.

That doesn't mean I won't ever have to do those Enablement and Tenacity parts of a project, but now I make better decisions as to when to take on those tasks. By taking the Working Genius assessment available at the link at GoodnessOverGreatness.com, **Working Genius gave me permission, as well as the language, to not feel lazy.** you can discover your strengths and dive deeper into how to make the most of your strengths. After you take the assessment, write your results below.

Working Genius

_____

_____

Working Competency

_____

_____

Working Frustration

_____

_____

What tasks am I consistently doing that are in my areas of Competency or Frustration?

_____

_____

_____

What are my next steps toward working more in my areas of Working Genius?

_____

_____

_____

The DISC Index

The DISC index leans more towards a behavioral assessment than VIA Character and Working Genius. The test measures your levels of Decisiveness, Interactiveness, Stability, and Caution. It also helps you better understand how you interact with others to determine how you normally respond and communicate.

The original idea for DISC comes from the work of Dr. William Moulton Marston, who believed behavior and communication are connected. Oddly enough, Dr. Marston not only wrote the book used to develop the DISC assessment, but he also created the lie detector and Wonder Woman and her lasso of truth.[16] He obviously looked for ways to communicate truth in every avenue of his life.

The areas with your highest numbers on the DISC Index indicate the behaviors you revert to when you start to feel stress. Understanding this allows you to be more natural and gives you better results with less effort, especially when working with others. For instance, if you score high in both the Interactive and Stability areas, your behaviors tend to be more people-oriented, while those who score higher in the Decisive and Cautious areas enjoy more task-oriented activities. On the other side of the scale, if your strengths fall in both the Decisive and Interactive sections, you're probably an extrovert, while those who lean toward both Cautious and Stability dimensions are more Introverted.

Erik's DISC

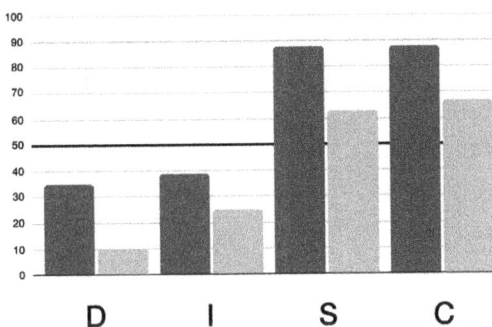

Caution and Stability rank highest on my scale, putting me on the introverted side of the square. These two areas influence my natural style the most. I appreciate security and occasional sincere words of affirmation. I like specific details related to my responsibilities, and I have an "everything in its place" preference.

Whether you're self-aware or not, we all become adaptive when we become conscious of others watching us or when we try to fit in. The DISC Index also provides this information so we can become more cognizant of our behavior. My adaptive style is the way I think I should behave rather than the way I naturally behave. This means sometimes I collect too much information and get bogged down in the details during decision-making.

I also have unique strengths based on the way these four behavioral styles relate to each other. I take my responsibility seriously and am generally patient when working with a team. I'm not an extremist and consider potential trouble spots others might miss.

I know all of these things about myself, in large part, thanks to DISC. Do you already have insights like these about yourself? Have you been able to make use of a tool like DISC in your own growth yet? If not, check out the link to the DISC assessment at GoodnessOverGreatness.com and record your results below

My DISC Results   **Rank 1-4**

    Decisive   _____

    Interactive   _____

    Stability   _____

    Cautious   _____

Do I lean more toward task-oriented or people-oriented projects for fulfillment?

_____

What next step will I take to use my natural abilities to their fullest?

_____

_____

What next step will I take to improve my communication skills in my weakest areas?

_____

_____

Develop an Awareness of Your Strengths

I've looked at many assessments over time and feel like these are the simplest to take and understand. I like the way these three round each other out by helping us see our character strengths, our working strengths, and our communication strengths. When we learn how to use the information we glean from these assessments with a team or in our personal life, our impact grows exponentially. Learning to put our strengths to work for us and integrate them as tools with co-workers and people we interact with speeds up our own growth as well as the growth of those around us.

Most people can become successful at anything they practice long enough, but is that really good for us? If you find yourself in a position where people think you are great but you feel miserable, it might be time to explore these assessments so you can become self-aware and embrace your true strengths and giftedness. Before you move forward, take a minute to understand your own strengths. As you develop increased awareness, you'll start to see the places you come on too strong with those characteristics. Because they make us feel comfortable and confident, it's easy to overdo it and become annoying. You'll also be equipped to give yourself permission to pass off those things that drain you and recognize traits in others, so you understand how to work with them better.

Awareness of strengths helps us see that many things we see as stressors give others energy. Things we consider boring or mundane may be someone else's sweet spot. Every position is necessary, and if we focus on strengths, we'll find the jobs we enjoy and be able to share those things we don't enjoy doing with the people who have the strengths to accomplish them best.

CHAPTER SEVEN

DRAW A ROADMAP

Goals are good for setting a direction,
but systems are best for making progress.

—James Clear

Now that you've refined your Reasons and identified your Reality, it's time to create a Roadmap—a system or plan to ensure you reach your destination. In his book Atomic Habits, James Clear tells us, "You do not rise to the level of your goals. You fall to the level of your systems." Suppose you have a strong desire to be fit and healthy. You set goals for yourself to be at a certain fitness level by the end of the year. Being aware of your desire is amazing! However, if you really want to succeed, ask yourself, "What excites me about that goal?"

If fitness is your goal, your motivation might be to live longer or keep up with your children or grandchildren. You might just want to be healthier. These are beautiful intrinsic motivators. Everyone needs them.

Now that you have your Reasons—to get healthier and spend quality time with your family—and your Reality—if you don't make a change, you'll be using a walker before you retire—the next step is to set up a system to help you succeed. To paraphrase James Clear, if you don't have and follow a Roadmap, you will fail.

In our fitness scenario, you need a schedule that takes you to the gym or a walking trail, and it has to be a commitment that you won't compromise. Your system for fitness will also need to include a plan to eat healthier. What does your shopping cart look like when you check out? You might need to create a system that skips the junk food aisles.

It's an Inner Journey

Regardless of our goals, in order to achieve them, we each have to create a clear Roadmap and gradually develop habits that will either guarantee success or help us see our goal isn't truly part of our reality.

One of the main points to remember as you begin this trek through Goodness over Greatness is that this is an inner journey. It's not designed to end in accolades or achievements (even if you get those along the way); however, the positivity and meaning you find on the Goodness Journey will make your life feel like an adventure.

It's vital to keep our eyes open for the Greatness Traps. The Goodness Journey doesn't promise a life of ease. Instead, it offers fulfillment and peace. However, as I've mentioned, avoiding the Greatness Traps requires a shift in mindset. Moving from destructive to constructive thinking will help us when the external trappings tempt us to sacrifice our path to peace.

Positive Psychology

The last twenty to thirty years of psychology have been built on an idea forged by Abraham Maslow in the 1950s. Martin Seligman, Christopher Peterson, Mihaly Csikszentmihalyi, and others have promoted, collaborated on, and developed the concept—something we call Positive Psychology.[17] This branch of the field focuses on character and building a life of meaning.

Too often, we hear people say, "I just want to be happy." Unfortunately, happiness, as opposed to joy, is a fleeting emotion because it's based on circumstances. It doesn't matter how much self-aware-ness we've developed or how well we've defined our reality; we're going to have bad days. Illness will still hit our fami-lies. Accidents will happen. We have no control over these day-to-day incidents.

We have the power to build our character and create a mindset of well-being that can withstand the storms of life.

On the other hand, we do have the power to build our character and create a mindset of well-being that can with-stand the storms. In fact, I've found hundreds of sources, in addition to the testimony of my own life, that say we can experience joy and peace in the face of adversity. We don't have to be happy about what's going on around us to keep a positive perspective about life.

This mindset is wrapped around five distinct zones that form the acronym PEACE[IP].

- Purpose
- Energy
- Appreciation
- Confidence
- Engagement

Shifting to a focus on PEACE allows you to live life to the fullest. Leading from the inside-out with positive psy-chology puts you in a position to steer yourself in a better direction as well as more effectively guide those you've been entrusted to lead. So let's explore the five areas of a life full of PEACE.

Purpose

Identifying your Reasons and Realities and understanding your strengths lay the foundation for knowing your purpose. Those first few exercises of our journey allowed us to shed the burden of everything well-meaning parents, teachers, and other influences prescribed for us. All those "shoulds" can be a tremendously heavy weight. When we know our purpose and abandon the voices from the past, we can find amazing freedom.

You may discover one or two of those voices from your childhood were on the right track. Some people are good at seeing us from the inside out. However, understanding our Reasons and Reality allows us to claim the purpose as our own rather than pursue it out of commitment to those voices.

Some people start with a sense of purpose but get sidetracked by the Greatness Trap of achievement. I've worked with entrepreneurs who have put ten to fifteen years into their businesses only to discover they don't like their job. Achievement at all costs took them off the Goodness Journey of progress with purpose. Maybe they found themselves seduced by the idea of growing. Perhaps the numbers game sucked them in—how many employees do you have, what's your annual revenue?

These people need to hit pause for a moment and reflect on the source of their peace and joy. What part of the day brings the most meaning to life? Sometimes getting back to the basics of their business and delegating the parts of their day that fall outside their purpose takes care of the discontentment. Other times, the entrepreneur finds it's time to sell and begin again.

Your core values and faith or spirituality create a strong groundwork for your purpose as well. Ask yourself a few reflective questions to help make certain you're working within your purpose

- Is your Goodness Journey calling you to volunteer somewhere or spend more time raising your children?
- Will growing your business strengthen those values?
- If you woke up tomorrow and someone let you know you were free to do anything you wanted, what would be the thing that would make you jump out of bed?

Without this sense of meaning, we feel like our lives lack direction. Take a few minutes and turn back a few chapters to review your strengths and values. Plan to revisit these every quarter or so. At the beginning of our journey, it's as if we're trying on these strengths and core values to see how they fit. They're like a jacket that needs a tailor. Some will fit well and others will simply need adjustments from time to time. A few folks may even need to buy a brand new jacket. Those who discover they never truly shed those expectations from others often

Without this sense of meaning, we feel like our lives lack direction.

need to start from scratch. But the more you grow, the clearer the purpose of your Goodness Journey becomes.

Energy

Knowing our purpose and acting on it positively affects our emotions, and those who experience joy, gratitude, and hope naturally have more energy. But this goes beyond noticing things and being thankful. In order to harness this emotional energy, we have to be intentional about cultivating an optimistic mindset.

Prior to the late 1800s, scientists believed the adult mind couldn't be changed or molded. When Adolf Meyer introduced the idea of a regenerative brain in the 1890s, he faced ridicule from his colleagues. Today, few dispute the concept of neuroplasticity—the theory that a person's experiences and thought patterns can reshape the brain.[18]

It's really amazing the way the mind works. Your brain has the capacity to create new neural pathways and modify existing ones depending on your behavior, experiences, and environment. The more you use your brain in a certain area, the more neurotransmitters are released, creating stronger communication paths between neurons. For instance, when you learn a new skill, the region of the brain that controls that skill grows.

This means you have the power to transform and renew your mind. Do you tend to be pessimistic, finding a way to look at things in the worst possible light? One first-century writer said, "Whatever is true, noble, right, pure, lovely, admirable, excellent, or praiseworthy, focus on these things."[19] Though he didn't understand the human mind like we do today, he realized that when we practice optimism, it makes a difference. Now we know finding the good in all things makes those neurons that produce joy and peace fire at the same time and eventually develop a physical connection.[20] Our brains are astounding!

Another of the Greatness Traps will force you to look only for the negative aspects of your business or your life so you can fix them. The Goodness Journey invites you to capitalize on what's going well. Your repeated positive (or negative) thoughts form new neural pathways or strengthen existing ones. And the positive ones give you the energy that comes from those praiseworthy emotions to empower you to lead from the inside out.

Negative motions weigh heavily on us. Scientists agree it takes three positive experiences to counteract one negative experience.[21] This means in order to maintain the energy from positive emotions, we need to activate positivity triggers. These can be as simple as recognizing things we should be grateful for or making heart-to-heart connections with important people in our lives.

Consider grabbing a notebook and doing some writing every evening before you go to bed. Answer these three questions each night:

1. What are you grateful for today and why?
2. What were your wins today—even if they seem too small to mention?
3. What upcoming milestones are you anticipating? How will you celebrate? Your celebration might be as simple as coffee with friends or as elaborate as a party.

Your brain also needs nutrition, sleep, and physical activity. It's hard to stay positive when you're hungry or all you've had to eat is chips and a cola. And you've probably experienced the side effects of not getting enough rest. We all work too late and get up too early from time to time. And while you might think this only robs you of physical energy, sleep, a balanced diet, and regular movement help us handle stress, giving us more mental energy as well.

Sleep might be one of the most difficult things for entrepreneurs to take hold of. We can find all kinds of advice on how many hours of sleep you need each night. But these don't take into account things like having three children or an infant. No one asks how many times you wake up at night because you're in pain or your hormones have gone crazy.

Our personal sleep needs differ just as much as our ability to sleep. Instead of comparing our sleep to the person who gets nine hours of sleep or being jealous of the guy who only needs four, we need to work within our own realities. Grade your sleep on a scale of one to ten—one being the worst sleep ever, ten meaning you wake up feeling completely rested and rejuvenated. The amount of sleep doesn't matter. Instead, ask yourself, "Where am I on a scale of one to ten with my sleep habits?" Go ahead and circle that number.

1   2   3   4   5   6   7   8   9   10

Next, unless you circled a nine or ten, decide what number you'd be satisfied with in your present circumstances and circle that number. Too often, we aim for ten; however, life doesn't always give us that gift. Rather than feel bad about ourselves because we can't reach perfection, let's work to reach something satisfactory. Give yourself permission to take naps and keep your expectations realistic.

You might not be able to get up and run before work like your best friend, but that doesn't mean you can't find a way to exercise. You might be able to improve your nutrition habits by eating six small healthy meals a day so you don't get hungry as easily. Perhaps you need to pack your lunch more often or see a nutritionist to develop a plan for the best things for you to eat. Your body has different needs than your peers. The key is to set goals and create a system to help you reach that next level.

Appreciation

The energy we derive from a healthy brain and positive emotions naturally leads to Appreciation. Your new neural pathways begin to see things in a different light. We appreciate our own strengths rather than envy our neighbor's. Appreciation moves us into a place of contentment. We're able to enjoy the moment. This doesn't keep us from moving forward. Staying where you are because life is adequate is complacency. However, when we appreciate the little things in life, we recognize our blessings, and instead of trying to keep up with the neighbors, we simply want to move toward being the best we can be.

Appreciation also gives us deeper and more meaningful relationships. It removes the Greatness Trap of putting recognition over relationships and keeps us on the Goodness Journey of impact through connection. In a world of remote work and online learning, it's easy to have fifteen video calls and convince ourselves we've done a lot of relating. While I appreciate the fact we can have co-workers and clients from around the world, this virtual environment our culture has created will never replace the face-to-face connections we experience in person.

When I was involved with hiring at my agency, I emphasized that because we're a fully remote company, the new team member needed to find a gym, church, or some community-based group to be involved in regularly. Humans need accountability and the opportunity to relate outside of work. The conversations over coffee or during a workout allow us to build and strengthen our relationships.

On top of that, appreciating yourself gives you permission to set boundaries where necessary. When we allow someone to abuse or take advantage of us, we aren't doing them or ourselves any favors. We can appreciate a person's strengths and recognize that they hold us back. Generally, when we need to create a boundary, we're also acknowledging that we aren't able to help them become the best version of themselves either.

Confidence

When you find a person with Purpose, Energy, and Appreciation, you'll discover someone who is developing Confidence. Some people paint a negative picture of confidence. They don't think it can co-exist with goodness. But they confuse confidence with the Greatness Trap of arrogance.

Accomplishments and accolades have the potential to feed confidence as well as arrogance. The difference is whether or not you've chosen Goodness over Greatness. Arrogance chases the idea of being better than everyone else and sits on the throne of Destructive Success. Too many entrepreneurs find out when it's too late that their business has been consuming them. They get so caught up in the victory and the adrenaline of winning, they miss their kids growing up. It's not until their spouse asks for a divorce that they look at the calendar and realize it has been eight years since their last real vacation.

> **Accomplishments and accolades have the potential to feed confidence as well as arrogance. The difference is whether or not you've chosen Goodness over Greatness.**

Confidence, on the other hand, is built on recognizing strengths and having a purpose. It balances self-fulfillment with self-control and develops with integrity and rich relationships. Unlike arrogance, confidence simply wants to be better today than it was yesterday, even if yesterday was already pretty solid.

We reach a place of contentment because we don't need to be at the same place in life as someone else. This Goodness Journey isn't a one-size-fits-all. My journey might be vastly different than someone else's.

One person might have a rapid and tremendous career but no spouse or kids. Another could have the best family life while they slowly build their business. A third person rose to the highest level in her business and managed to balance a tremendous family life, too. Which one would you consider the most accomplished? Which should be the most confident?

What if all three paths demonstrate Constructive Success? I've seen people in each of these scenarios with extreme self-awareness, a knowledge of strengths, beautiful core values, and well-developed PEACE. Confidence doesn't envy, judge, or try to keep up with someone else.

Failure might hit confidence in the gut and shake it for a moment. But because true confidence doesn't depend on the world's definition of greatness, it soon sees those defeats as temporary setbacks. Or better yet, confidence often sees failure as a necessary ingredient to getting to the next level.

Engagement

One of the biggest Greatness Traps is distractions. Every area of our lives has the potential to accompany us on the Goodness Journey when we remain completely present. In our relationships, Engagement means we put our phones in our pockets or leave them in our car while we play a game or have a conversation. It means we turn off work notifications when we're having dinner or helping with homework. And the most difficult part of engagement is keeping our brain from wandering off while our body goes through the motions of being present.

The Pixar movie Soul shows us a fun example of staying engaged. When jazz pianist and middle school teacher Joe Gardner's soul gets separated from his body because of an accident, it goes into another realm that includes a space called "The Zone."

Every soul enters the Zone through whatever creative thing or act of doing feeds them. Then they get lost in the Zone, enjoying their creative outlet. Joe's path to the Zone was a piano. Every time he touched the keys, he became so engaged with his creative side that he lost track of time and even forgot he wanted to get his soul back in touch with his body.

Mihaly Csikszentmihalyi describes this heightened state as flow. He called it a complete absorption in the current experience, and he named it flow because in his interviews, he discovered that when athletes, musicians, and artists reached periods of optimal performance, they felt their work simply flowed out of them.

When we become fully engaged, we reach a point where nothing matters to us except the task at hand. Flow causes us to become so involved in an activity that we will continue to do it even at great cost. We can't help ourselves; we do it for the sake of doing it.

Flow fits naturally with Goodness over Greatness because it's most easily achieved by people who walk the Goodness Journey with ease. You see it in a variety of ways:

- People who find more joy in the process than the end result.
- People who are curious, purpose-driven, and persistent.
- People who are less concerned with fame, wealth, or power and more dedicated to their passions and interests.[22]

In the business world, entering flow can increase your productivity. Athletes often call it getting "in the zone." You lose self-consciousness. I call it the ultimate state of engagement or your sweet spot. Usually, to access a flow state, you have to be doing something challenging, hopefully using your strengths and skills. It should be something you enjoy but not anything too relaxing, and it has to be something that requires complete focus. We become so engaged, we don't have enough attention left over to give in to feeling bad, hungry, upset, or uncomfortable.

Being present in this way has proven to help guard against depression and burnout, and fortunately, we can become just as engaged with our family and friends as we do with our strengths and our businesses. On top of all that, people who experience this level of engagement have a higher sense of well-being.[23]

Creating Your Roadmap

After you've defined your Reasons and Reality, it's time to choose the route to your destination. Every person's Roadmap will include a shift in mindset and a path that includes PEACE; however, because of our unique strengths, values, circumstances, and relationships, each Roadmap will be different.

In our high-speed world, your journey may feel painfully slow, but some of us need to walk to become the best version of ourselves. The exercises and techniques you find in this book are meant to help you give up the constant striving and move into a Rhythm that allows you to counter the rough parts of the road and maybe even enjoy them.

The most beautiful route can be difficult to determine and maintain without an accountability peer, coach, or mentor. Engagement also means we need others to travel with us. Fortunately, now that you've completed the exercises up to this point, you can begin to set points on your Roadmap so you know which way to head next. Let these questions help you plot your Goodness Journey.

First, write down the things you discovered about yourself as you read. Let's start with PEACE in mind:

What is your Purpose?

_____

What emotions and activities feed your Energy?

_____

Which relationships do you Appreciate the most?

_____

Where would you rank your Confidence level? From little confidence at one to tremendously confident at five.

1   2   3   4   5

How could you increase that number?

_____

How would you rank your Engagement level? From distracted to totally engaged?

1   2   3   4   5

How could you increase that number?

_____

How do these five areas refine your definition of reality?

_____

_____

_____

_____

Now that you know your goals and have an idea of where you are now, you can begin to create a system to move you forward. You might want to use a pencil so when you revisit these questions every few months, you can make changes as needed. Each time you refine your answers, you'll add pixels to your picture until you have a clearly defined reality that lets you lead even more effectively from the inside out.

What system and habits would help you achieve the goal that excites you the most?

_____

_____

_____

_____

CHAPTER EIGHT

FINDING YOUR RHYTHM

*Our greatest fear should not be of failure
but of succeeding at things in life
that don't really matter.*

—Francis Chan

Unfortunately, even after we define our Reasons, identify our Reality, embrace PEACE, and create our Roadmap, we'll encounter Greatness Traps that linger along the Goodness Journey. If we're not prepared for them, they can keep us running in place. You may have been in one of those snares before. Something didn't feel right. Boredom or frustration froze you in your tracks. And when you were finally able to move, you felt like you were on a treadmill getting nowhere.

Most often, these feelings come because we're working outside our strengths or living in someone else's reality. Stagnation also occurs when we strive for things that don't line up with our core values. Some people feel lazy, others call themselves procrastinators. But really, most are just stuck on their road to success.

So far, I've asked you to write, assess, and self-reflect, but we're done with the pondering. It's time to start implementing so we can get into a Rhythm and move from treading water to swimming with freedom.

It's Time to Leap

I have a riddle for you. Four frogs sit on a log. Three decide to jump off. How many are still on the log? I like asking this question when I'm speaking. Some say one. Others say none because the three jumping off would knock the last frog off.

But what's the correct answer? Four. You're probably thinking that's impossible, but here's the catch: *deciding* to jump off and actually *taking the leap* are two different things.

Maybe you or someone you know has decided to run a marathon this year. That's a wonderful ambition, but unless you get up tomorrow and run a mile, you'll be as likely to run a marathon in a year as you are today. Another person may read twenty-four personal growth books in the next twelve months, but if they don't put anything they read into practice, they're still frogs on a log.

> *Deciding* to jump off and actually *taking the leap* are two different things.

It's time to take everything we've discovered about ourselves and make our move. Return to the system you set up in the last chapter. Refine it, set deadlines, build habits, and let your system work for you. If a fear of failure holds you back, it might help to remember that if you don't make the first move, you've already failed.

This is the point where many people need a coach, mentor, or accountability partner to keep them motivated. Don't feel like you have to do this alone.

Brock Purdy was the official "Mr. Irrelevant" in the 2022 NFL Draft—the very last pick. But before he went to the 49ers® training camp, the young man enlisted the help of Tom Gormely, a physical therapist with CORTX Sports Performance. Gormely and CORTX's quarterback coach, Will Hewlett, worked with Purdy for months before he became San Francisco's starter, the first rookie to win against Tom Brady, and an NFL 2023 MVP finalist. Purdy believes he would have already topped out without the coaching he received from Gormely and Hewlett.[24]

As I mentioned earlier, coaching isn't limited to athletes. Football coach Bill Campbell turned his attention to executive coaching after he went into business. He worked with many Silicon Valley visionaries. Apple's Steve Jobs and Amazon's Jeff Bezos both invited Campbell to coach them on their road to success.[25] [26]

Goodness over Greatness Compass[IP]

When we step into this area of doing, it will be tempting to return our focus to achievement and accolades. If you haven't already made a solid decision to make Goodness the foundation for your Greatness, you'll easily get caught up in the doing and lose who you are in the work.

Greatness goals will soon turn into the amount of work you have to do, how much recognition you can get, and the number of metrics you can achieve. Goodness goals, however, force you to stay focused on the Non-negotiables, Sustainable Growth, Essence, and Well-Being (NSEW). Roadmaps and compasses work well together. When you examine every goal under the compass of NSEW, you can be sure Greatness Traps haven't encroached on your Goodness Roadmap. This allows us to create a comfortable Rhythm in our day-to-day—a plan that keeps us engaged but allows us to stay on the path.

- **Non-Negotiables** serve as your true north. These are the core values and principles you refuse to compromise, no matter the external pressure or temptation. Just like a compass always points north, your Non-Negotiables provide unwavering direction. Every shift in your path requires a check-in:

- o Does this decision align with what matters most to me?
- o Am I honoring my integrity, or am I making choices based on fear or external approval?
- o If I continue in this direction, will I still recognize myself?

- **Sustainable Growth** ensures that your pursuit of success doesn't come at the cost of your long-term well-being. Like a well-paced marathon, meaningful progress happens in steady steps. If your plan demands relentless hustle without space to recover, reflect, or enjoy the process, it's likely steering you toward burnout instead of fulfillment. Ask yourself:

- o Is this goal pushing me forward at a sustainable pace?
- o Am I making room for both progress and rest?
- o Will this enhance or drain my mental, emotional, and physical health over time?

- **Essence** moves us to the East side of our compass, reminding us to stay connected to who we truly are rather than chasing an image or external validation. Success means nothing if we lose our sense of self in the process. When evaluating your path, consider:

- o Am I making this choice because it resonates with me, or because it looks good to others?

o Does this goal reflect my deepest values and aspirations?

o Am I building a life that feels like *mine* or one that just looks impressive from the outside?

- **Well-Being** balances our compass. True success isn't just about achievements—it's about how you *feel* while pursuing them. If your goals constantly leave you exhausted, anxious, or disconnected from the things that bring you joy, they may not be worth pursuing. Prioritize well-being by asking:

o Is this goal allowing me to show up fully in my personal life?

o Am I taking care of my mental, emotional, and physical health as I pursue success?

o How will this decision impact my happiness and fulfillment long-term?

By using this compass, you ensure that any Greatness you reach remains anchored in Goodness. When each goal is filtered through the lens of **Non-Negotiables, Sustainable Growth, Essence, and Well-Being,** you can move forward with confidence, knowing that success isn't pulling you away from who you are—it's reinforcing it.

Let's Do Something

Are you ready to leap? Let's take a moment to evaluate our goal and create a checklist that requires action. Create additional copies of this for each goal. You can also find a template in the resources section of GoodnessOverGreatness.com.

1. What is your goal?

2. What strengths will you use to achieve this goal?

3. How does it align with your core values?

4. How does this goal fit with your current reality?

5. How will working toward and achieving this goal affect those around you?

6. What are your next five steps?

   ☐ _____
   ☐ _____
   ☐ _____
   ☐ _____
   ☐ _____

CHAPTER NINE

A RHYTHM THAT INCLUDES GIVING BACK

Whoever renders service to many
puts himself in line for greatness—
great wealth, great return, great satisfaction,
great reputation, and great joy.

—Jim Rohn

Fear that leads to hoarding might be the biggest Greatness trap. Some people never feel like they have enough. Every penny gets invested, and they look at gifts mostly as ways to reduce taxes.

However, when we transform our mindset to one of Goodness, we set in motion a beautiful ripple effect. One of my favorite parts of the Goodness Journey is that it includes giving back.

It may seem like we're completely focused on ourselves; however, this concept of Goodness over Greatness always touches those around us. We will naturally influence everyone we come in contact with, and their lives will affect spouses and children, whose behaviors will influence their communities. You may have no idea who you inadvertently touch as you build Goodness within yourself.

The Tiny
Wellbeing Rippple

Recreation of "The Tiny Wellbeing Ripple" by PositivePsychology.com

In the 1960s, meteorologist Edward Lorenz discovered that tiny butterfly-scale changes to his computer weather model produced significant and unpredictable changes in his forecast. It's no wonder the weather predictors have such a difficult time getting it right!

NASA uses Lorenz's theory to control outer space trajectories. They discovered tiny bursts of fuel have the power to steer spacecraft more accurately. It's this theory that allowed them to meet up with the Giacobini-Zinner comet.

The movie *The Butterfly Effect* took Lorenz's theory one step further, a leap many have made through the decades.

Leading from the inside out allows us to be an influence that causes more sunny days than rainstorms.

Our every action creates a stir as gentle as the movement of a butterfly wing, but that breeze has the potential to bring social and emotional hurricanes or sunny days.[27]

Leading from the inside out allows us to be an influence that causes more sunny days than rainstorms.

Five Levels of Leadership

Inside-out leadership isn't taking authority to force change because you're the boss. This kind of demanding personality creates Destructive Success, if success at all. Constructive Success comes when you lead with your strengths, core values, and a sense of well-being.

A true leader influences, inspires, and guides others through their actions and example. They want to empower others while remaining grounded in their own values and have the ability to balance ambition with compassion and humility.

John Maxwell defines five levels of leadership.

- **Position**: Maxwell calls the lowest level of leadership Position. You're appointed to be a leader. People only follow you because they believe they have to. If you abuse this level, you become that authoritative boss. On the other hand, if you use it to your advantage and put humility, empathy, integrity, and relationships in the forefront, you can quickly move to the second level.

- **Permission**: This level is based on relationship. People give you Permission to lead because you connect with them. You see small ripples of influence because you make people feel appreciated. They trust you because they see your honesty and can sense you care. So, they follow you to the next level of leadership.

- **Production**: This leader knows how to get things done. People moved you into this level because they trusted you, but they continued to follow because you helped them achieve group goals. In fact, if you're interested in helping them reach their goals as well, you'll quickly move to the next level.

- **People Development**: At this level, you begin to create new leaders. Inside-out leadership kicks in as you invest in others. This is where you begin to see big ripples as the people you mentor begin to move into the permission stage of leadership.

- **Pinnacle**: This is the most challenging level to attain. It requires hard work as you invest yourself in others for the long haul. You stick with them and focus on growing yourself at every level.[28] This level gives you the greatest satisfaction, and because you've put Goodness first, you can finally experience true Greatness.

Leave a Legacy

Matthew Henry, a great Christian commentator, once said, "Goodness makes greatness truly valuable, and greatness makes goodness much more serviceable." Making greatness valuable is one of my pinnacle goals. A famous Bible passage says, "If I speak in the tongues of men or of angels, but do not have love, I am only a resounding gong or a clanging cymbal. If I have the gift of prophecy and can fathom all mysteries and all knowledge, and if I have a faith that can move mountains, but do not have love, I am nothing. If I give all I possess to the poor and give over my body to hardship that I may boast, but do not have love, I gain nothing." [29] I want any greatness I achieve to make huge ripples that out-last me. And I want the same for you.

This idea of legacy can be achieved by making sure your greatness keeps the HEIR in mind.

- Humility – Goodness over Greatness is rooted in humility. This means working toward our goals always focuses on ripples instead of recognition. Humble leaders focus on their own growth first and the growth and well-being of others second. Acknowledgment and accolades are never primary in legacy-focused greatness.
- Empathy – Empathy considers others every step of the way. When things go wrong, empathy looks at things that might have influenced the person who became the broken spoke in the wheel. This part of our acronym feels for others and motivates us to move from hoarding to giving.
- Integrity – Honesty goes a long way with most people. When we own our mistakes and people know they can trust our word, they want to follow us.
- Resilience – When we work within our strengths and core values, we equip ourselves to withstand the hard times. Goodness over Greatness does not guarantee success with no problems, but it creates a Rhythm that puts us on the path to the kind of leadership that creates a lasting impact.

Leadership from a place of scarcity, fear, or greed makes it impossible to leave a legacy because you're afraid to let go of anything. On the other hand, as Matthew Henry said, when you reach greatness through the path of goodness, your goodness becomes much more serviceable.

Greatness has the potential to finance your goodness. It can make your ripples go further faster.

Greatness has the potential to finance your goodness. It can make your ripples go further faster. Millard and Linda

Fuller used the millions they attained on the road to greatness to fund the goodness of their core values. Without greatness, they couldn't have started Habitat for Humanity. The ripple effect of Millard's philanthropic efforts has improved housing conditions for more than twenty-nine million families.[30]

Charles Feeney has been called a hero by Warren Buffett and Bill Gates. In 1982, the billionaire secretly transferred the bulk of his wealth to Atlantic Philanthropies. Until his death in 2023, no one who received help from his generous giving was permitted to announce where the funds came from. He disliked the lifestyle of the ultra-wealthy and lived out the end of his life in a rented apartment in California. The billionaire used his influence to facilitate the peace process in Northern Ireland and secure life-saving medicine for HIV victims in Africa. Feeney allowed his goodness to surpass his greatness, but it was his greatness that funded his endeavors.[31] [32]

Dave Thomas, founder of Wendy's, used his greatness to create the Dave Thomas Foundation for Adoption.

Countless athletes, recording artists, and other celebrities have proven that a foundation of goodness gives greatness the potential to leave legacies that will live for generations after we're gone. And while the funds they accumulated because of their greatness allowed them to create their charities and give big, goodness drives the efforts.

What Is Your Inspiration?

A drive for philanthropy added to your Reasons, Reality, and Roadmap can often inspire you as you get into a steady cadence on the Goodness Journey. When we start the journey with ME—understanding your Reasons and Reality and developing PEACE as you create your Roadmap—we have the potential to rise to a level of greatness that moves past WE to THEY.

Think about who this THEY might be.

- If you had significantly more than you need, what would you do with the excess?
- What charities touch your heart?
- What hardships would you like to alleviate?
- Who would you like to help?

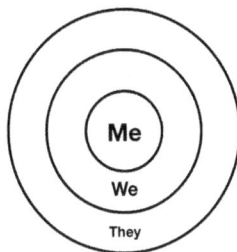

Once you have answers to these big questions, ask yourself how you can start *today*, no matter how big or small that financial support is.

_____

_____

_____

_____

_____

_____

CHAPTER TEN

NEXT STEPS

There is no greatness
where there is no simplicity, goodness and truth.
—Leo Tolstoy

Now that you have the basic steps, I hope you'll make your first move within the next week. If you haven't taken the assessments yet or accessed the other resources I mentioned, then your first action should be visiting GoodnessOverGreatness.com.

I don't want this book to simply give you a new outlook. I want it to set you in motion. I'm hoping you'll revisit the worksheets in these pages on a regular basis so you can see how much you've grown and reevaluate where you want to go.

The field of positive psychology is continually growing and developing. Over the last century, scientists have completely shifted their theories about the way the brain changes and regenerates. Your ability to know yourself and apply these concepts will grow right along with it. But what will you do to make sure you keep up?

Find Someone to Challenge You and Keep You Accountable

I know I've said it several times already, but to expedite this process, a coach will be your biggest asset. Let's face it, we don't change well on our own. You've probably tried books or online courses, but they don't quite get you to your goal. An executive coach might be exactly what you need.

Some people ask where a coach fits in the picture. Should he or she walk ahead of you, clearing the way, or follow behind, cheering you on? In truth, the best coach walks with you. It's the coach's job to help you find your footing along the way.

How would it change your organization if the leaders experienced a shift in their ability to influence and empower those they lead? What if they could achieve greater results and find better ways to solve problems? A coach can help your team increase their leadership skills and improve engagement in the company.

You may only need a coach for a season, or you might have a specific agenda you want to get moved across the finish line. If you feel like you're carrying a burden you can't get rid of or are facing an obstacle you can't get past, a coach is probably your best next step.

We Grow Better in Groups

Meeting with a group of like-minded leaders from a variety of industries to go through concepts and content allows you to learn at a pace and on a scale most can't keep on their own. When you can see principles from the perspective of so many others, it speeds your growth.

On top of learning, a group setting allows you to put the principles you've learned into action, and action is the key in bringing Goodness over Greatness to life.

There are many groups like this that you can consider. Some are large by design, while others are strategically small, limited to just eight to twelve participants. I've been a member of a number of groups like this since 2010, and they've brought me immense value.

At Built on Purpose, our Growth Groups^{IP} meet weekly or bi-weekly, depending on the group. They create a time and space for business owners to meet with a small group of other owners who can truly relate to the complexities of owning a business. After all, most owners don't have a specific person they're accountable to, nor do they have a place where they can share openly about their biggest wins and their lowest lows. Meeting with a group of people who understand where you are can prove extremely valuable.

One-on-One Coaching With Me

I don't simply share these steps as principles. They've been instrumental in getting me where I am today. I spent years building websites in my first company and then shifted my attention to operations and culture development. This process helped me uncover my strengths and core values and pushed me toward the moves I shared in the first chapter.

Leaving my CEO seat, COO position, and then leadership entirely freed me to do the thing that makes me jump out of bed each morning—one-on-one coaching. I love helping owners think differently about what work could be. And I enjoy helping them build the business and the life that takes them from surviving to thriving.

Whether you choose to work with me or not isn't my main focus. More than anything, I want you to see how the quality of your life can drastically improve with this simple Goodness over Greatness mindset shift. I also want you to consider the value of having a good coach in general.

You might already know coaches you can connect with. Whether it's me or someone else, strike up a conversation to learn more about how a coach can expedite your journey. Is it time to rediscover your professional purpose and craft so you can enjoy the freedom I've found by learning to lead from the inside out?

Okay, you've made it to the end, or perhaps you have just made your way to the beginning. However you choose to look at it, it's time to make goodness your foundation so you can rise to true greatness and leave an amazing legacy. Lasting leadership starts here.

APPENDIX

GREATNESS TRAPS

On the Goodness Journey, there are exits that seem worth taking. Promises of recognition, success, and significance lure us off course. But these exits often lead us to places that look impressive from the outside and feel hollow on the inside.

I call them **Greatness Traps**.

They don't always look bad. In fact, they usually look smart, strategic, and even admirable. But the danger is this: the more time we spend in them, the further we drift from what makes us whole. These traps can sabotage our well-being, compromise our values, and ultimately keep us from becoming the person we actually want to be.

Here are some of the most common Greatness Traps I've seen—and fallen into.

1. **Recognition over Impact**

   What it looks like: Chasing applause or status instead of doing the work that matters.

   Why it's dangerous: Validation becomes your compass, and you start shaping your identity around how others see you.

   Where it shows up: Social media, article features, public accolades.

2. **Busy over Meaningful**

   What it looks like: Constant activity that gives the illusion of progress.

Why it's dangerous: You sacrifice depth for speed and run the risk of burnout.

Where it shows up: Hustle culture, overloaded calendars, zero-margin weeks.

3. **More over Enough**

What it looks like: Constant upgrading. Always wanting the next level.

Why it's dangerous: Satisfaction stays just out of reach. Enough is never enough.

Where it shows up: Lifestyle creep, business scaling, compulsive goal-setting.

4. **Image over Integrity**

What it looks like: Projecting what others want to see instead of being who you are.

Why it's dangerous: You become a character you created to be liked, not someone you respect.

Where it shows up: Personal brand building, leadership personas, curated vulnerability.

5. **Comparison over Connection**

What it looks like: Measuring your life against others rather than living your own.

Why it's dangerous: It isolates you and makes others your competition instead of your community.

Where it shows up: Peer benchmarks, social media scrolling, envy masked as ambition.

6. **Control over Trust**

What it looks like: Clutching every decision, believing you're the only one who can do it right.

Why it's dangerous: You become the bottleneck and keep others from growing.

Where it shows up: Delegation issues, founder-dependence, team frustration.

7. **Comfort over Calling**

   What it looks like: Staying safe in roles or routines that no longer serve you.

   Why it's dangerous: You stagnate. You stop becoming.

   Where it shows up: Careers, relationships, unfinished dreams.

8. **Speed over Depth**

   What it looks like: Prioritizing fast results over lasting impact.

   Why it's dangerous: What you build may not endure.

   Where it shows up: Business growth, leadership decisions, rushed creativity.

9. **Action without Intention**

   What it looks like: Doing just to be doing. Checking boxes without a compass.

   Why it's dangerous: You may be successful in the wrong direction.

   Where it shows up: To-do lists, crisis mode, nonstop execution.

10. **"No One Can Do It Like I Can"**

    What it looks like: Believing you're indispensable.

    Why it's dangerous: You rob others of ownership and burn yourself out.

    Where it shows up: Leadership transitions, micromanagement, trust gaps.

11. Ego-Driven Achievement

What it looks like: Achieving to prove something, not to serve something.

Why it's dangerous: Your identity gets hijacked by your need to win.

Where it shows up: Competitive spaces, personal branding, fragile confidence.

12. Turning Weaknesses into Strengths

What it looks like: Spending energy trying to be great at everything.

Why it's dangerous: You neglect your strengths and reduce collaboration to compensation.

Where it shows up: Performance reviews, development plans, imposter syndrome.

13. Recognition over Relationships

What it looks like: Seeking applause more than intimacy.

Why it's dangerous: You win crowds and lose connection.

Where it shows up: Fame, social leadership, attention economies.

14. Arrogance after Accomplishment

What it looks like: Thinking success makes you immune to feedback.

Why it's dangerous: You stop learning and stop listening.

Where it shows up: Executive roles, thought leadership, "arrival" mentality.

15. Distractions (Shiny Object Syndrome)

What it looks like: Constant pivoting toward the next big thing.

Why it's dangerous: You trade traction for novelty and leave value half-built.

Where it shows up: Startups, content strategies, project overload.

16. Growth for Growth's Sake

What it looks like: Scaling because you can, not because it's strategic.

Why it's dangerous: You lose sight of your purpose and people.

Where it shows up: Revenue targets, hiring sprees, or expansion plans without purpose.

17. Saving That Becomes Hoarding

What it looks like: Reluctance to invest, give, or enjoy what you've earned.

Why it's dangerous: Fear masquerades as wisdom, and you forget what the money was for.

Where it shows up: Retirement planning, wealth management, generational legacies.

Remember, each of these traps is a fork in the road. And while they may offer short-term benefits, they rarely offer long-term fulfillment.

The path of goodness doesn't avoid greatness, but it grounds it. And when you find yourself in a trap, it doesn't mean you've failed. It means you have a choice. A chance to pause. Reflect. And reorient yourself back to what matters.

Back to who you really are. Back to goodness.

ENDNOTES

1   Maxwell, John C. *The 21 Irrefutable Laws of Leadership: Follow Them and People Will Follow You.* HarperCollins Leadership, Revised & Updated edition, 2007.

2   https://www.merriam-webster.com/dictionary/good

3   *History.com.* "Cornelius Vanderbilt." Updated March 26, 2020. https://www.history.com/topics/19th-century/cornelius-vanderbilt

4   Minton, Rob. *Dividend and Real Estate.* "How the Vanderbilt Family Lost Their Fortune." Accessed November 11, 2024. https://dividendrealestate.com/vanderbilt/

5   Andrew Wilkinson. *Never Enough: From Barista to Billionaire.* Matt Holt Books, 2024.

6   Mark 8:36

7   Nouwen, Henri. *Spiritual Direction: Wisdom for the Long Walk of Faith.* Harper Collins: NY. 2006.

8   Hamilton, Alexander. "The Farmer Refuted, &c., 23 February 1775," *Founders Online, National Archives,* https://founders.archives.gov/documents/Hamilton/01-01-02-0057. Accessed 9 April 2025.

9   *IMDB.* "Captain America: The First Avenger Quote." Accessed November 15, 2024. https://www.imdb.com/title/tt0458339/quotes/

10 Bonderanko, Peter. *Britannica.* "Enron Scandal." Updated October 24, 2024. https://www.britannica.com/event/Enron-scandal

11   Davies, Dave. *NPR*. "Short-term profits and long-term consequences — did Jack Welch break capitalism?" June 1, 2022. https://www.npr.org/2022/06/01/1101505691/short-term-profits-and-long-term-consequences-did-jack-welch-break-capitalism.

12   *Conscious Capitalism*. "Why is Consciousness the Key?" Accessed November 15, 2024. https://www.consciouscapitalism.org/story/feature-why-consciousness-is-the-key

13   Philippians 4:8

14   Houston, Parker. *LeadYouFirst*. "Great Leaders Know Their Strengths and Place Others in Their Strength Zones." January 21, 2021. https://leadyoufirst.com/great-leaders-know-their-strengths-and-place-others-in-their-strength-zones/

15   Sullivan, Dan. *The 80% Approach*. Strategic Coach: Toronto, Canada. 2013, 2015, 2018.

16   *Wikipedia*. "William Moulton Marston." Accessed November 20, 2024. https://en.wikipedia.org/wiki/William_Moulton_Marston

17   *Psychology Today*. "Positive Psychology." Accessed November 23, 2024. https://www.psychologytoday.com/us/basics/positive-psychology.

18   Lamb, Susan. *National Library of Medicine*. "Neuroplasticity: a century-old idea championed by Adolf Meyer." December 9, 2019. https://pmc.ncbi.nlm.nih.gov/articles/PMC6901269/.

19   Philippians 4:8

20   *Brainfutures*. "Neuroplasticity 101. Accessed November 23, 2024. https://www.brainfutures.org/neuroplasticity-101

21   Robinson, Bryan E. Ph.D. *Psychology Today*. "10 Ways to Apply the 3-to-1 Positivity Ratio." October 17, 2020https://www.psychologytoday.com/us/blog/

the-right-mindset/202010/10-ways-apply-the-3-1-positivity-ratio.

22   *DesignDash.* "As a Creative, Do You Have an Autotelic Personality?" December 30, 2023. https://designdash.com/2023/12/30/as-a-creative-do-you-have-an-autotelic-personality.

23   Hope-Jones, Eleanor. *Flown.* "In the zone: the science behind flow states and how to spark productivity." April 20, 2023. https://flown.com/blog/deep-work/in-the-zone-the-science-behind-flow-states-and-how-to-spark-productivity.

24   Martin, Angelina. *Yahoo Sports.* "How 49ers QB Purdy fixed key throwing issue before 2022 NFL draft." November 3, 2024. https://sports.yahoo.com/49ers-qb-purdy-fixed-key-010720455.html.

25   Metrosilis, Teddy. *The Process.* "The man who coached Steve Jobs." September 17, 2023. https://www.theprocess.news/p/steve-jobs-executive-coach-bill-campbell.

26   *Tech PE - Generating Alpha & Superior IRR.* "Leadership Lessons from Bill Campbell – The CEO Coach to Steve Jobs, Eric Schmidt and Jeff Bezos." June 24, 2020. https://www.zorian.com/leadership-lessons-from-bill-campbell-the-ceo-coach-to-steve-jobs-eric-schmidt-and-jeff-bezos/.

27   *APS125.* "Butterflies, Tornadoes, and Time Travel." Accessed November 29, 2024. https://www.aps.org/archives/publications/apsnews/200406/butterfly-effect.cfm.

28   Maxwell, John. *John C. Maxwell.* "The 5 Levels of Leadership." August 30, 2016. https://www.johnmaxwell.com/blog/the-5-levels-of-leadership1/

29   1 Corinthians 13:1-3

30   *Habitat for Humanity.* "Impact." Accessed November 29, 2024. https://www.habitat.org/emea/impact.

31   Mento, Maria D. *The Chronicle of Philanthropy.* "Charles Feeney's Legacy: $8 Billion in Giving,

and a Bold Example. October 10, 2023.
https://docs.google.com/document/d/1oR_
h2ddHNJAit6fjgHVgvS9dkGWQQs8OgJrAo_CXbvk/
edit?tab=t.0.

32 *The Atlantic Philanthropies.* "Chuck Feeney." Accessed
February 14, 2025. https://www.atlanticphilanthropies.org/
chuck-feeneys-story.

ACKNOWLEDGMENTS

What do you even say after finishing your first book? I feel like giving shout-outs to everyone I know, because everyone has been so encouraging.

To my wife, Nikkie—you've been my biggest cheerleader and encourager. Thank you for believing in this book, and more importantly, in me. To Brady and Cade, your thoughtful birthday gifts—chosen with this book in mind—meant more to me than you probably realized. You reminded me that this wasn't just about finishing a book—it was about stepping into something bigger, something you both get to witness and be proud of.

To my sister, ~~Jerk~~ Laura Sue, and brother-in-law, Anthony—thank you for working alongside me at Built on Purpose and seeing where it could go. Mixing family and business can be risky, but I genuinely loved getting to work alongside you both.

To my mom and my mother-in-law: thank you for cheering as I worked on this. There's a kind of quiet strength that only moms bring, and I felt it the whole way through.

To my late father and father-in-law: I miss you both in a way words can't express. This book is dedicated to you, and I hope it would've made you proud.

To Tim Elmore and Sangram Vajre—thank you for launching *A Book in a Weekend* and creating the space that allowed me to take this idea seriously. That weekend sparked a fire. Mark Cole—your one-on-one coaching session was one of those conversations that sticks and stirs something deeper. Thank you for seeing and speaking into this project.

And to my Book in a Weekend cohort—what a gift it was to chase this dream together.

To Kary Oberbrunner and his incredible team—thank you for walking me through the wild world of publishing with grace, patience, and structure. And to Lynne Modranski—thank you for helping me wrangle all the ideas and shape them into something people can actually read. Your partnership made this real.

To my business partners at Focus Lab, Bill and Will—thank you for the support, but more importantly, for your friendship. And finally, to Versonya DuPont and Leslie Nelson—my first accountability partners—thank you for sitting with the very rough beginnings and encouraging me to keep going when the finish line felt miles away.

There are so many fingerprints on this book, and I wouldn't want it any other way. It may have my name on the cover, but it carries all of you in its pages.

With Gratitude,
Erik

ABOUT THE AUTHOR

Erik Reagan is an author, entrepreneur, coach, and award-winning speaker with multiple certifications through DISC, Working Genius, Executive Coaching, and more. In 2010, he took his first steps into the entrepreneurial world and built Focus Lab, a world-class branding agency with an award-winning culture.

While developing Focus Lab, Erik discovered a passion for leadership and executive coaching. He quickly realized this pursuit was what motivated him to get out of bed in the morning. He established a leadership development firm called Built on Purpose, where he empowers entrepreneurs to drive change from the inside out.

Erik also carries his passion into speaking engagements. He loves inspiring others to cultivate growth, resilience, and peak performance in themselves and their businesses.

He lives with his wife, daughter, and son in southeast Georgia, where they love to read, laugh, and play with their dogs together.

Connect with Erik at ErikReagan.com

Goodness over Greatness isn't just a book. It's a way of living.

Looking for a keynote that challenges the status quo and sparks meaningful reflection?

Discover the power of inside-out leadership. From Greatness Traps to the Goodness Compass, I'll guide your audience through the counterintuitive mindset that unlocks freedom, fulfillment, and sustainable success.

GO FURTHER, TOGETHER.

Entrepreneurs, you're not meant to do this alone.

Join a Growth Group—a hand-selected cohort of business owners who meet biweekly for meaningful discussion, personal growth, and accountability.

You'll grow your business, your leadership, and your impact—**without losing yourself in the process.**

READY TO LIVE THIS OUT?

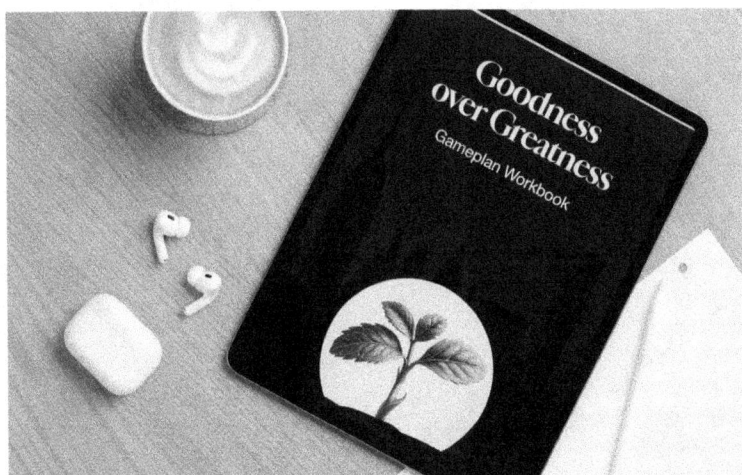

Leverage the companion workbook for momentum.

The Goodness over Greatness Gameplan Workbook will help you turn insights into habits.

With tools like the Inside-Out Wheel, Greatness Trap Inventory, and the NSEW Compass worksheet, you'll design a life that's rooted in your values and rich with meaning.

Rediscover your purpose.
Redefine your path.

I help high-performing entrepreneurs rediscover joy, alignment, and ownership over their lives—not just their business success.

If you're ready to recalibrate your business, leadership, or life around what really matters, let's connect. Schedule a no-pressure call to learn about what one-on-one coaching can do for you.

To learn more about coaching, visit
GoodnessOverGreatness.com/coaching